Litany of the Morrígna

Litany of the Morrígna

A hundred names for the Daughters of Ernmas, from the Irish lore

By Morpheus Ravenna

Concrescent Press

For information contact:
Concrescent Press, Richmond CA, USA
info@Concrescent.net

ISBN: 978-1-958359-03-7

Introduction

This little book is an offering of devotion, both to the Morrígan and her sisters, and to the poetic tradition that holds their myths and texts. In these pages, I present a Litany of a hundred names and epithets of praise to the Daughters of Ernmas—the Irish war goddesses Morrígan, Macha, Badb, and Némain. Following the Litany, I offer commentary on each of the epithets, giving its context and background in the Irish source literature, as well as what the language of the epithet tells us about its meaning.

The first version of the litany was created in the spring of 2020. During the lockdown period at the start of the Covid-19 pandemic, I had more time than usual for creative projects, since as a tattoo artist I couldn't work. At the same time, the daily anxiety of existing during a deadly pandemic drove me to focus more on devotional practice, seeking the security and support of the gods. In my daily devotions, I found myself wanting a litany of praise to recite. I remembered a beautiful devotional I had attended just a few weeks prior, held by my good friend Ali Montgomery, a devoted priestess of Sekhmet, in which we had recited a hundred holy names of that fierce desert goddess. I thought to myself, "There must be at least a hundred epithets of the Morrígna in the Irish literature," and with that, this Litany began.

There are, it turns out, well more than a hundred. The early Irish literature these are sourced from is a rich well of poetry, full of evocative, vibrant images and powerful emotion. In creating this Litany, I combed through texts from the Dindshenchas, the Mythological cycle, the Ulster tales, as well as annals, histories, glossaries, and a variety of other kinds of texts. A wealth of epithets spilled out from these stories—so many that I needed to curate them. This Litany isn't exhaustive of all the ways the Morrígna are described in these tales. It represents my harvest of a hundred names that I felt drawn to from the literature. The epithets are grouped according to the goddess they describe, beginning with the Morrígan, Macha, Badb, and Némain, and finishing with a short section of epithets for the Daughters of Ernmas as a collective. Within each section, the order of the epithets is organic: I placed them according to what sounded poetic to my ear and gave the Litany a pleasing rhythm.

I also want to acknowledge the part of devotional community in deepening my relationship with the Litany and helping me to develop the commentaries on the epithets. The first version of the Litany was published online and began to be used in devotionals in the Coru Cathubodua Priesthood and associated community. Soon after that, my beloved friend Vyviane Armstrong led a series of community discussions on a Discord server in which we explored each of the epithets in more depth. These conversations inspired me to look more closely at their literary contexts as well as the original Irish material from which they were translated. I'm grateful for the path those conversations led me down, and for each of the participants who took part. Some of them are quoted in this book.

Along that path I spent a lot of time with language research, feeling my way among webs of meanings spun by the authors of the Irish texts. Irish medieval literature is full of layers and gleams of multiple meaning. I learned just how much of the English translated material from the Irish medieval literature consists of what I call Creative Victorian Translation—or in my less charitable moments, Victorian Fuckery. Translation is profoundly shaped by the translator's worldview. Spending time with the original language material offered an opportunity to shape a new understanding of these epithets, and in that process I changed quite a few of them from the form in which they were first published online. As a Litany meant to be used in devotional life, it should be a living document that feeds and is nourished by our lived values and understandings of the gods.

One more final note about language. The source material I drew from for this project spans a wide historical period within which the form of the Irish language changed. It includes material in Old Irish from the early medieval period to Middle and even some Modern Irish from the Early Modern period. As such, the spellings of words can vary quite a bit. When I'm quoting a source, that source's spellings are retained. When I'm speaking in my own words, I usually use whatever spelling is most common for a word or name.

I hope this work may be of value in your own devotional life. The Litany can be used both in prayer and contemplation. Speaking the names offers praise, and reading about them stirs devotion in the heart; both bring us closer to the Great Queens. Perhaps this work might also inspire others to create similar litanies of devotion for the gods we hold dear.

Litany of the Hundred Names
of the Morrígna

Morrígan

1 of the fairy-mound of Crúachan
The shape-shifting goddess
Terror of night
Great queen
5 Mighty Morrígan
Able to destroy
Woman poet
Red woman with a red mantle
Owner of kine
10 Surpassing nobility
White, red-eared heifer
She who stands fast
Who comes to us
from the edge of a pillar
Nine loosened tresses on her head
15 Dangerous woman
Her pleasure is in mustered hosts
Crone, one-eyed and half-blind

Cunning raven-caller
Daughter of Delbaeth
Black bird upon a branch
Lean, nimble grey-haired hag
Foundation of sorcery
Horror of the cave of Crúachan
Furious the sarcastic laugh
she laughs
Eldritch shape
The Dagda's wife
Slippery, black eel
She who is at the guarding of death
Shaggy, russet she-wolf
Sower of strife and dissension
She hovers over
the points of weapons
Many are the spoils she washes
Battle-eager, always-ungentle queen
Morrígu who brings victory

Macha Red-haired

Queen by virtue of her strength

The impetuous, powerful one

Macha, the very shrewd

By whose command
was the fort of Emain raised

Fierce for glory

Greatness of pride

Bright Grian, the sun of womankind

Swifter than the king's horses

First death of the people of Nemed

Greatness of wealth

The warrior's fair wife

Noble daughter of
redweaponed Aed

Great with child

The raven of the raids

Whose crop is the heads of men
that are slaughtered

Gentle Macha

She who radiates excellence

Red Badb

Terrible fury

Blue-mouthed, loud-croaking crow

Slaughter upon the host

She who darkens the sky
with phantoms

The pale one

Ferocious of reply

60 Hag of sorcery,
blind in the left eye

Fiery red-lipped scald of war

Blazing torch

Demon of the air screaming
from the rims of shields

Incitement to combat

65 She whose longing is for fire

Red-mouthed sharp-beaked
scaldcrow

Headless one

War-goddess
crying among the corpses

Lone woman casting evil eye

Bitch

Fire of judgment

Red woman on the edge of the ford

Chosen for iron-death

Brooding scald crow

Ravenous, red-clawed carrion

She who relates great deeds

War-goddess
shrieking above the ford

Cry that foretells blood

Sharp-tongued, curse-speaking

White lady

Badb who shall destroy

Némain
the war-goddess

Venomous

Wife of war

85 Who brings confusion on the host

Warlike disturbing wife of Néit

She of the wounds of war

The praise-worthy woman

Wild and grim

90 Némain of prophetic verses

Law-giver

Némain of the anguish-cry

Noble daughters
of Ernmas

Wellsprings of enchantment

95   Specters and phantom queens

Compassers of death
by the sword

Battle-crows

By whose shrieks
a hundred warriors die of terror

Sources of bitter fighting

100   Sorceresses of the Tuatha Dé

Morrígan

Morrígan
of the fairy-mound of Crúachan

This epithet comes from the *Táin Bó Regamna*, a story in which the Morrígan encounters Cú Chulainn while she is transporting a cow: "I brought this cow out of the fairy-mound of Cruachan, that she might breed by the Black Bull of Cualnge, that is the Bull of Daire Mac Fiachna."[1] It's just one example of a pattern in which the Morrígan is frequently associated with "fairy mounds" or said to come out of them. The phrase "fairy-mound of Cruachan" here is translated from *sith Cruachan*, identifying the place as a *sith*, a word which means fairy hill, mound, or dwelling, or can refer to the Otherworld more generally.[2] Crúachan is the ancient name for Rathcroghan, the royal site of the province of Connacht in the west of Ireland. The *sith* of Crúachan refers to the cave also known as Úaimh na gCait (or the anglicized Oweynagat).

The use of the word *sith* for a cave may highlight the perceived similarity of megalithic mounds to caves: both enclose dark spaces which were felt to open into the Otherworld. These sites should perhaps be considered more as entrances or passages into a wider Otherworld rather than endpoints in themselves. Perhaps this aspect of the *sith* of Crúachan as a gateway helps explain why the stories show so many different Otherworldly creatures coming out of there: in addition to the Morrígan, the tales also tell of monstrous cats, giant pigs, werewolves, and frightening supernatural birds emerging from the cave.[3] The Irish Otherworld isn't a singular place; it comprises many, overlapping Otherworlds. The cave of Cruachan seems to be one which opens into an especially frightful or dangerous realm, as most of the creatures which emerge are seen as destructive or ominous. The Morrígan's close association with this cave places her in relationship to this family of frightful beings. In some manuscript versions of *The Triads of Ireland*, this cave is described as one of the "three darknesses of Ireland."[4]

The shape-shifting goddess

This epithet is drawn from a poem about Odras in *The Metrical Dindshenchas*, translated by Edward Gwynn: "in this wise came the shape-shifting goddess…"[5] It is part of a scene in which the herdswoman Odras has followed the Morrígan in order to recover a bull taken by the goddess. The Irish phrase that is the source of this translation is *ba samla día sóach*. Here *samla* is a ghost, apparition, or likeness.[6] *Día* is straightforward, a goddess. *Sóach* is quite obscure; it appears to be a form of the verb *sóid* or its verbal noun *soud*, "turning, changing."[7] A more literal translation of this phrase cited by eDIL is "the shape-shifting goddess was a phantom." The poetry here suggests an apparition that is in the motion of changing its shape.

The Morrígan is well established as a goddess who changes her shape—she appears in various places in Irish tales as a beautiful young woman, an old woman blind in one eye, a wolf, a heifer, an eel, and a crow or other black bird. It seems here that the fluidity of the act of changing may be hinted at. Perhaps one of the poems spoken by her can give us insight into this shifting. In a poem spoken to Cú Chulainn, she seems to describe her experience of shape shifting: "my great shaking released me/ so that I obtain a raven soul."[8] There is the sense of shaking loose from one shape in order to take on another.

This epithet comes from the 8th century poem *Reicne Fothad Canainne*. This poem contains some of the most evocative descriptions of the Morrígan in the Irish literature, and it's interesting that it is written as from the perspective of the dead. It's addressed by a warrior Fothad Canainne, to his lover, explaining that he has been killed in battle and so cannot meet her. He begs her to gather his things and hurry away from the battlefield, because the terrifying Morrígan is haunting the place:

> *Do not wait for the terror of night*
> *on the battle-field among the resting-places of the hosts;*
> *one should not hold converse with a dead man,*
> *betake thee to thy house, carry my spoils with thee!*[9]

The Irish text of the epithet is *aidche úath*, for which "terror of night" is a fairly straightforward translation. *Úath* is not simply the feeling of terror or horror, however, but is a word which refers to a class of spiritual beings sometimes called horrors: dreadful, terrifying supernatural beings who haunt battlefields, and are especially active at night. They are encountered in many other tales where they are not always associated with a goddess, so it is notable that this poem frames the Morrígan as one of these *úatha*.[10] It is interesting to think of terrors as beings; many folklore traditions about the psycho-spiritual condition known as sleep paralysis (or "night terrors") attribute the experience to visitations by spiritual beings. It is not uncommon to hear about contemporary people having encounters with entities like the Morrígan during episodes of night terrors.

This also calls to mind that one of the possible etymologies of the Morrígan's name traces the element *mor* (unaccented) to a root meaning "phantom," related to Germanic *mara* as in modern "nightmare." This is where the popular devotional epithet "Phantom Queen" comes from. Nowadays, this theory has fallen out of favor with linguists in favor of the one which traces her name to *mór*, "great," giving "Great Queen." However, in light of her association with specters and phantoms, even if "Phantom Queen" isn't the origin of her name, it's a very appropriate epithet.

Great queen

Great Queen is a direct translation of the Morrígan's name. Here, the first element is taken as *mór*, "great, big, mighty", and the second is *rígan*, "queen."[11] Some medieval texts which mention her preserve the initial accent in the spelling of her name: Mórrígan. The etymology of her name continues to be debated, and some still hold to the "phantom" etymology theory as mentioned in the previous epithet. Regardless of which may be the earlier or original meaning, when considering her lore, both are valid names or titles for her.

Great Queen is interesting in that it appears to be a title. In many instances when she is mentioned in early texts it's with the definite article: an Morrígan—"the Great Queen." I've sometimes wondered if this is to do with the folk custom of not directly naming spiritual beings who are powerful and potentially dangerous. This epithet also seems to connect her to a group of goddesses with related names, across a wide spectrum of different Celtic cultures. Alongside the Morrígan in Ireland, there is the medieval Rhiannon in Wales, and the older Iron Age Riigina in Britain and Rigana in Gaul.[12] These names are proposed to originate from an archaic *Rigantona, "Queen Goddess." Clearly, there is something perennial about the presence of goddesses concerned with sovereignty. While the Morrígan isn't necessarily a sovereignty goddess in the classical sense of directly embodying the sovereignty of the land, she seems to be engaged with sovereignty, especially with the contestation of sovereignty through martial conflict.

Mighty Morrígan

For this epithet, I return to the Odras poem in *The Metrical Dindshenchas*. Gwynn's translation intones, "There came to blood-stained Cruachu, according to the weird and terrible tale, the mighty Morrigan, whose pleasure was in mustered hosts."[13] In community discussions about this one, the descriptor "mighty" has sometimes elicited reactions to what can be perceived as gendered qualities—the notion that it might convey a sense of masculinized, "macho" physical power. Looking at the source language can help us unpack this.

The word which has been translated as "mighty" is *mórda*. This is a superlative of *mór* which as mentioned above, means "big, great," both in the sense of size and in the sense of scope and power. As a superlative, *mórda* carries the sense of the most exalted, majestic, noble; the utmost.[14] This epithet proclaims her the most exalted, the greatest-of-great queens. It highlights both her power and greatness, and at the same time seems to say that she is very herself, fully established in her power.

Able to destroy

I drew this epithet from *The Second Battle of Mag Tuired*. The Túatha Dé Danann are preparing for the battle and each of them are asked what powers they bring to aid in the struggle. The Morrígan says of herself, according to Elizabeth Gray's translation, "I have stood fast; I shall pursue what is watched; I will be able to kill; I will be able to destroy those who might be subdued."[15] An alternate translation by Morgan Daimler offers, "Pursue what was observed, pursue to strike down, I control bloody destruction."[16] The Irish source text appears to be arranged as a short poem, showing some of the alliterative and rhythmic features of *rosc* poetry:

ar-rosisor dosifius
dosselladh arroselus
ar-rosdibu nosriastar.

The phrase relating to destruction is from *díbaid*, "to destroy, annihilate," and *srían*, "control, check, restrain."[17] This conveys a sense that destruction is in her power, but it is a controlled power, calculated and intentional. One might also ask here what is the target of her destructive power. In a direct sense in the Mag Tuired story, the adversaries she is preparing to fight are the Fomoire. Further, the reason for this battle is that the Fomoire have acted as oppressors, causing hunger and deprivation, and it's for this reason they are being overthrown. So in a more broad sense, one can perhaps read her statement as "I am able to destroy adversaries of justice."

This epithet might encourage us to reflect on our relationships to destructive powers. I have often observed that the Morrígan has a great capacity for disruption. When she enters peoples' lives, there is sometimes a period of chaos where old patterns and limiting relationships can suddenly begin to crumble, and this can be very disruptive. Often there is a sense of destruction of harmful structures to make space for something new. I think in her destructiveness, she can be a liberator and a breaker of chains.

Woman poet

This epithet appears in the *Táin Bó Regamna*, a story in which the Morrígan encounters Cú Chulainn while she is transporting a cow, and when he tries to stop her, she threatens him and warns of his death. The epithet is a title she uses to introduce herself during this exchange. A. H. Leahy's translation is "I am a female satirist in truth;" the Irish word she gives is *bancháinti*.[18] In the Litany I've reproduced this as "woman-poet" but the title contains a more specific meaning, referring to a female poet who practices satire (*cáintecht*) outside of the legal system and who is therefore regarded as rather dangerous.

Irish law had a gendered view on this. Fergus Kelly writes: "The law-texts reserve particular odium for the illegal satirist who is female. In *Bretha Crólige* the *birach bríathar* (lit. 'one who is sharp with words') is classed along with the female werewolf and the vagrant woman." Religious institutions similarly found her deeply threatening: "according to *Fís Adomnán*, the *cáinte* is doomed to spend all eternity up to his waist in the black mires of Hell, along with sorceresses, brigands, preachers of heresy and other miscreants."[19]

In this passage, the Morrígan is identifying herself with werewolves, sorceresses, brigands, and miscreants—beings both socially and spiritually liminal. She is also identifying herself as someone with dangerous poetic skill and not bound by the legal system. She says, in effect, "Don't try me, because I'm not answerable to anyone, and I will cut you with word magic." It is a profound threat.

Red woman with a red mantle

Continuing with the encounter with Cú Chulainn in the *Táin Bó Regamna*, this epithet also appears in the same story. It is in one of the more complete descriptions of the appearance of the Morrígan in Irish literature:

Then they saw the chariot come before them, and one chestnut (lit. red) horse in it. The horse was one footed, and the pole of the chariot passed through the body of the horse, till a wedge went through it, to make it fast on its forehead. A red woman was in the chariot, and a red mantle about her, she had two red eye-brows, and the mantle fell between the two ferta of her chariot behind till it struck upon the ground behind her.[20]

The way in which everything about her is red is quite striking. The language that has been chosen is also interesting. The word usually used for a red-headed person is *ruad* (Modern Irish *rua*), a word customarily used for the naturally occurring tawny or brownish red of red hair, red fox fur, etc.[21] But that's not the word employed in this description. Instead, everything about her is *dearg:* blood red, a word more usually used for things that are a vivid or bright red, such as red-hot objects or fresh blood, or which can imply something being bloody.[22] Even her horse is that color. Red color in these tales can sometimes be an indicator of the Otherworldly. This scene in which everything about her is blood-colored and she rides behind a horse impaled on its own chariot pole creates an unnerving impression of a terrifying presence from the Otherworld.

The garment translated here as "mantle" is a *brat*, which is a type of simple cloak worn from very ancient times through into early medieval times, usually folded and pinned across the chest with a decorative cloak pin. There may also be an indicator of rank here, as the text mentions that her mantle is so long that it drapes over the chariot. This may be a statement about great wealth in being able to afford a luxuriantly long, vividly dyed cloak—an expensive status item to medieval people.

For this epithet, I've returned to the *Metrical Dindshenchas* poem about Odras. Speaking of the Morrígan in the act of enchanting Odras, the poem relates, "The owner of kine chanted over her, with fierceness unabating…"[23] The word Gwynn has translated as "owner of kine" is *agda*. This translation interprets the word as a compound of *ag*, "bovine animal, cow, ox."[24] However, I can find no other examples of this usage, and for that reason I think it might be a variant spelling of *ágdae*, "warlike, contentious."[25] In fact, this same word appears earlier in the poem, in a passage "according to the weird and terrible tale," where it's clear it does not refer to cattle. What this may be is a device often seen in early Irish poetry, where multiple layers of meaning are alluded to by the use of words that sound similar. A native speaker might hear both the direct meaning of warlike, and the meta-textual allusion to cattle which are the focus of the story.

Cattle were very important in early Irish society. They were foundational to a diet which centered on dairy and meat, and were a form of currency, a container of wealth, and a measure of status. Trade, ownership and movement of cattle were structural aspects of society. Tribes and petty kingdoms raiding each other was a way of life. Reputations were built on the deeds done in these raids, and sagas retold these tales. One of the most prolific genres of Irish story is the *táin*, or "cattle raid."

The Morrígan appears in many stories that involve raids or movements of cattle, in addition to the tale of Odras. For example, a druid named Tulchaine wanted to marry a fairy woman named Dil who had a special cow linked to her by being born on the same day. To marry Dil, Tulchaine needed to capture the cattle herd, so he prayed to the Morrígan for help in this, and was successful.[26] The Morrígan also acts behind the scenes to ensure that the calf is born who will grow up and become the Brown Bull, whose theft is the motivating trigger for the Cattle Raid of Cúailnge.[27] She engineers that whole war starting a generation ahead, using cattle.

These stories provide a fascinating insight into the Morrígan and cattle. To her, cattle are more than wealth; they are chess pieces—they are social levers for manipulating events. This is particularly interesting in light of the cosmological significance of cattle. Many Irish myths that relate to the creation of the landscape involve cattle or cattle divinities, such as the cattle goddess Bóann, and the combat of the two bulls, the Donn Cúailnge (Brown Bull of Cooley) and the Finnbennach (White-Horned Bull) which shapes the landscape of Ireland in the *Táin Bó Cúailnge*. The Morrígan's role seems to be in instigating cosmological conflict as part of a cycle of destruction and renewal.

Surpassing nobility

The first version of this Litany that I published online had this epithet as "surpassing beauty," which comes from Cecile O'Rahilly's translation of the *Táin Bó Cúailnge* (First Recension version). It is from an episode in which the Morrígan offers to help Cú Chulainn: "Cú Chulainn saw coming towards him a young woman of surpassing beauty, clad in clothes of many colours."[28] She presents herself as the daughter of a king, bringing great wealth and a tempting offers of a marriage alliance which he rejects. The scene has been interpreted in various ways; one of the more persuasive interpretations, I think, is that she is testing him to see if he can be distracted from his mission or "bought off" with wealth and status.

The different ways this story has been interpreted are themselves revealing of the cultural lenses and assumptions that each reader brings to a reading of early texts. Much has been made of the Morrígan's supposed "seduction" here. Cú Chulainn himself reacts as if this is seduction, saying "It is not for a woman's body that I have come." However, looking in more detail at the description of her, what she is offering is more about power than sex. The phrase translated as "surpassing beauty" is *delb roderscaigthe furri*, where the descriptive word is *roderscaigthe*. That is, *ro,* an intensifier, and *derscaigthe* which means "distinguished, excellent, pre-eminent, superlative."[29] This word does not actually reference physical beauty or sexuality; its meanings all have to do with status, rank, and comparative excellence. "A semblance of surpassing nobility was on her" would be a clearer translation here, or perhaps "She appeared as the most noble of nobles." Even the description of clothes of many colors is a marker of wealth and status, in a time when many of the brightest colored dyes were only affordable to the rich. The translator has made the same mistake many modern readers make, and the same mistake Cú Chulainn made, in interpreting the Morrígan's presence in terms of sexual attractiveness rather than as a power move. This is why I've changed the Litany to use "nobility" instead of "beauty."

White, red-eared heifer

This epithet comes from the *Táin Bó Cúailnge*, in the scene in which the Morrígan attacks Cú Chulainn in several animal shapes during one of his fights. One of the shapes she takes for this fight is that of a cow: "So the Morrígan came there in the guise of a white, red-eared heifer accompanied by fifty heifers, each pair linked together with a chain of white bronze."[30] The First Recension version of the *Táin* describes her slightly differently, as a "hornless red heifer."[31]

The color word in both versions is *derg*, a bright or bloody red. I have touched on the idea that people and animals with the color red can often be markers of Otherworldliness. On its own, the description of a white cow with red ears might not indicate an Otherworldly creature, because this phrase also describes a traditional, heritage breed of Irish cattle which are still kept today: the Irish Moiled.[32] This breed goes back at least to the early medieval period, usually hornless and red or white in color, and typically with red about the ears.

Here, it's clear that this is no ordinary cow, as the text tells us it's a guise adopted by the Morrígan. She also has markers of Otherworldliness not only in the red color, but also in that she appears with a herd of cattle linked in pairs by white bronze chains; this pair-chaining motif is also something that shows up with animals from the Otherworld, such as the birds hunted by Cú Chulainn leading to his being struck down with a fairy curse or "wasting sickness."

One might ask why the Morrígan would choose the heifer as a shape to enter for combat; since most people would not typically think of a milk cow as a martial animal. Irish folklore and literature is full of stories in which usually harmless animals take on threatening, Otherworldly forms, such as the iron-beaked venomous sheep who defeat a whole Munster army in the *Siege of Knocklong*.[33] It seems to be a folkloric motif in which the familiar becomes frightening as the Otherworld intrudes into ordinary life.

She who stands fast

For this epithet, I've returned to *The Second Battle of Mag Tuired*, where each of the Túatha Dé Danann are asked to state what powers they bring to the battle. "I have stood fast; I shall pursue what was watched; I will be able to kill; I will be able to destroy those who might be subdued."[34]

The Irish text, again, is this:

ar-rosisor dosifius
dosselladh arroselus
ar-rosdibu nosriastar.

Another perspective contributed by Caróg Liath suggests *ar-rosisor* as "my purpose will be to stand fast," from the verb *ar-sissedar*, "to stay, stand fast, remain."[35] It is followed by *dosifius*, from *do-seinn* "pursue, drive, hunt."[36] The Morrígan both stands fast and pursues; holds her ground and when opportunity opens, pursues to strike. These phrases are followed shortly by "I control destruction" in the last part of the statement.

I think it's interesting to contemplate this phrase in light of her role in *The Second Battle of Mag Tuired*. She operates as a kind of catalyst around which the tides of battle turn. At a point when great slaughter is taking place on both sides, she appears and gives a poem of incitement, and immediately the battle breaks and the Fomoire are driven to the sea.[37] She seems to stand fast as a point of strength around which events turn.

Who comes to us from the edge of a pillar

This epithet is found in the poem *Reicne Fothaid Canainne*, describing the Morrígan who has come to the battlefield among the dead. Kuno Meyer's translation includes the line "She has come to us from the edge of a pillar, 'tis she who has egged us on; many are the spoils she washes, horrible the hateful laugh she laughs."[38]

It seems likely that this line refers to pillar-stones, i.e. standing stones. These monuments are referenced quite often in early Irish literature, such as druids standing atop them to chant their spells during battle; and Cú Chulainn performing ogham magic using them.[39] The Morrígan has also associated herself with pillar-stones when she perches atop one to give a warning while in bird form: "the Mórrígan, in the form of a bird which perched on the pillar-stone in Temair Cúailnge and said to the bull: 'Does the restless Black Bull know…"[40]

These standing stones are a visual presence all over Ireland; many of them would have been present when these sagas were being written. They were used as boundary markers and as funerary memorials, among other things. Medieval people would likely have associated them with the past and with the dead; perhaps it is this association that the poem speaks to when it says that the Morrígan comes to us from the edge of a pillar.

This epithet has more to tell, however—the language contains a poetic double-entendre. The Irish line is: *Donárlaith do bil óige*, in which *bil óige* is "edge of a pillar." But *óige* isn't the typical word used to refer to pillar-stones; in the stories that mention them, they are usually called *coirthe*. The translator has taken *óige* as a variant spelling of *áige*, which does mean pillar, but more so in a poetic sense, as one might say someone is your pillar of strength.[41] *Óige* also means a young person or a warrior.[42] And *bil* is "edge," a word often used in the context of the rim of a shield, but also more generally to mean a border or boundary.[43] So the double-entendre here is "she has come to us from a boundary stone," and "she has come to us from the weapon of a warrior."

This is very interesting in light of the poem context: it's said by a dead warrior who has been killed in battle. The Morrígan is coming to claim the dead—she has literally come to them from the weapon of a warrior. At the same time, it also suggests the liminality of pillar stones as boundary markers, and seems to say something about the Morrígan as a liminal being, emerging from a borderland.

In *The Second Battle of Mag Tuired*, the Morrígan meets the Dagda for a marital tryst. "He saw the woman at the Unshin in Corann, washing... There were nine loosened tresses on her head. The Dagda spoke with her, and they united."[44]

The word used to describe her hair is *trilis*, which means a tress or plait of hair, or the sections of hair that make up a plait.[45] The adjective is *taitbechtai*, meaning "opened, dissolved, loosened, untied."[46] This line has been translated fairly directly, but what a glib reading might overlook is that it seems to be describing the untying of plaits or loosening of a dressed hairstyle. That is to say, she has had her hair in nine plaits or tresses, and has loosened them for this meeting.

I have wondered if this is an oblique reference to the practice of warrior braids. Early Irish literature mentions braided hairstyles in association with membership in warbands or a warrior life-path in a couple of places. The tale of the warrior woman Creidne mentions this as a descriptive detail associated with her entry into warrior life:

> Then Creidne went on the warpath to despoil her father and her step-mother on account of her sons being outside their proper kindred. She had three bands of nine men with her on the warpath. She used to wear the hair of her back plaited. She would fight equally on sea and on land. Hence she was called Creidne that was a fenid.[47]

Braided hair is also mentioned in the description of the trials of the Fianna, which youths would undergo to test their worthiness to join the warband. These tests included an ordeal of pursuit, during which the youth must be able to navigate through the woods, wearing plaited hair, and without a lock of hair dislodged from its plait:

> The fourth condition: no man was admitted into the Fian until, having his hair plaited, he was sent through several woods

with all the Fian in pursuit of him with a view to wounding him, while he got but the odds of a single tree over them, and if they overtook him, they would wound him...
The sixth condition: no man was admitted among them if a branch of a tree in the woods unloosed from its plait a single braid of his hair.

If the braiding of the hair in a certain way may have been a habit adopted by warriors, this could convey a layer of significance to the Morrígan's loosening of her hair for her marital tryst with her husband, the Dagda. It seems to suggest softness, the setting aside of warrior ways or letting down her guard for this moment of intimacy.

The number nine seems significant as well. In many Celtic cultural contexts, things in threes imply a wholeness, the extension of something to totality or throughout all the three realms. Three-times-three seems to be a magnification of this. Perhaps the nine tresses is the storyteller's way of conveying that her hair is the *most*—a great volume of epic, impressive hair, signifying great beauty and power.

Dangerous woman

This epithet appears in the encounter of the Morrígan and Cú Chulainn in the *Táin Bó Regamna*: "Then he saw that she had become a black bird upon a branch near to him. 'A dangerous woman thou art,' said Cuchulain."[48] The word Leahy translates as "dangerous" is *doltach*, which comes from the noun *dolud*, meaning "hurtful, oppressive, damaging, distressing, disruptive."[49] This description seems to align with the way she is presenting herself in this scene as a poet, using language that points to being an outlaw satirist, someone who operates outside of the legal system regulating the use of satire, and therefore dangerous.[50]

The epithet is Cú Chulainn's reaction to recognizing her identity. He is someone who has committed to a warrior life path at this point, knowing that he's fated to die young and by violence, and having actively chosen this way of life. His reaction here might suggest that this is a moment where the reality of his choices is setting in; he is recognizing the cascade of fated events he is embarked on, and this is his startled reaction to the realization.

There's more here. This epithet relates to a place-name which is identified *Dindshenchas*-style in the story, which indicates that there was a story tradition attached to the location. Returning to Leahy's translation: "'A dangerous woman thou art,' said Cuchulain. 'Henceforward,' said the woman, 'this clay-land shall be called *dolluid* (of evil,)' and it has been the Grellach Dolluid ever since." A *grellach* is a bog, swamp, or loamy place, so this is a place name meaning something like "dangerous/oppressive bog."[51] In other words, this is a big power move on her part. He calls her a dangerous woman, and her reply is, essentially, "Bitch yes, I'm a dangerous woman, and to make sure you never forget it, this place will forever be called the Bog of Doom." That's a flex!

Her pleasure is in mustered hosts

For this epithet, I've returned to the *Dindsenchas* poem for Odras. Gwynn's translation gives: "There came to blood-stained Cruachu, according to the weird and terrible tale, the mighty Morrigan, whose pleasure was in mustered hosts." The Irish is *ba slóg-dírmach sámda*. Here the poem is talking about the mustering of many troops or armies together: *slóg*, "army, host, company;"[52] *dírmach*, relating to many troops.[53] Her feeling in this environment is *sámda*, "peaceful, restful, calm, at ease."[54]

This is a remarkable statement about her. In the company of many armies, mustering together, she finds her ease and peace. She is at home here. It could also be read as, "Her serenity was in gathering armies." The poet may be drawing an intentional contrast here. Armies generally aren't mustered for peace; they're mustered for war. For many people, the environment of a gathering of armies might not be so restful; it might signify a time of impending conflict, an environment of activity and preparation, of tension or a calm before violence. This is where she's at peace.

Another way of looking at it was contributed by Rob Preece, speaking about what it might be like in a seasonal time of mustering:

> *Armies would be mustered annually even in peacetime… New bodies would be brought into the war and and old ones told they could stand down. There would be a lot of drinking, boasting and telling tall stories of previous exploits, not the formal bardic recitals but personal stories. Mustering would be very festive because it's the lord or king's supplies everyone is living off rather than their own. As the spears were counted, confidence would rise. The appointment of people into the command structure would generate a ton of gossip. In short a great time to be under arms… The worry comes once the host have marched off or taken to boats and the reality of final goodbyes floods in like black water.[55]*

Crone, one-eyed and half-blind

This epithet is quoted from the First Recension of the *Táin Bó Cúailnge*. After Cú Chulainn and the Morrígan have wounded each other in combat, she appears in this shape, milking a cow. "While Cú Chulainn lay thus in great weariness, the Mórrígan came to him in the guise of an old crone, one-eyed and half-blind and engaged in milking a cow with three teats."[56] She gives him the milk to restore his strength, and in return she gets his blessing to heal her injuries. She is wearing this look as a disguise, and it's a description that could have come from many different text sources. Sometimes the Morrígan, sometimes Badb, this hag figure represents a sort of archetype worn by these war goddesses at moments of their choosing.

She is *i n-delb na sentainne caillige*: in a shape of an elderly woman.[57] *Caillech* has a literal meaning of "veiled" but idiomatically refers to older women, those who have "taken the veil," or who seem malevolent, like a hag or witch. And she is *cáech losc*: *cáech* is "one-eyed," but also has a secondary meaning of "veiled or mysterious,"[58] and *losc* is "infirm, disabled in one leg," (often translated using what would now be considered ableist language such as "crippled, lame.")[59] These descriptions seem to lean into the belief which is conveyed throughout many stories in the Irish tradition that injury or disability to one side of the body meant that part was active in the Otherworld, and beings of this kind were themselves liminal and in a sense straddled the border between worlds. She is also milking a cow with three teats; perhaps an indicator that this cow isn't an ordinary cow either.

It's interesting that she's described as wearing this shape as if in disguise, but the only part of her appearance that is actually a disguise is perhaps looking like an old woman. In fact Cú Chulainn has just wounded her in the eye, the ribs, and the leg, and it's these same injuries she's seeking a blessing of healing for from him.

Returning to the Odras *Dindshenchas* poem once again, Gwynn's translation reads: "The envious queen fierce of mood, the cunning raven-caller, brought off with her the bull that lived in miry Liathmuine."[60] The Irish phrase is *in fiachaire fathach*. *Fiachaire* doesn't have a direct equivalent in English because it refers to a role that doesn't exist in modern English-speaking worlds. It relates to a domain of seership through reading omens in the behavior of birds, and specifically ravens. The word is a compound of *fiach*, "raven,"[61] with *aire*, "chief, noble, lord, master."[62] It could be translated as "raven-master;" eDIL also has "bird-seer," although "raven-seer" would be more precise.[63]

This title is a relict from ancient times when there seems to have been a tradition of divination by bird-augury. A medieval Irish text records this, called *Prognostications from the Raven and the Wren*, about how to divine by the behavior of ravens and wrens; this skill is called *fiachairecht*; "raven-mastery" or "raven-lore."[64] The text describes the various behaviors one may observe in ravens and what each might signify. Quite a few of these behaviors are described in reference to interior spaces, suggesting perhaps that there may have been a tradition of performing this type of divination with domesticated ravens kept for the purpose.

This type of divination with ravens seems to be what the poet wants us to see as one of the Morrígan's skills. She is described as *fathach*, "wise, possessed of knowledge" particularly of a mystical kind.[65] Another translation of this epithet could be "wise raven-seer." It is hard not to think of that poem where the Morrígan describes her process of shapeshifting as "taking a raven soul"—perhaps that could also involve calling a raven to yourself.

Fiachaire has persisted in the language into Modern Irish, where it refers to a weather forecaster, that is, someone who forecasts conditions by watching the sky![66]

In a poem in the *Lebor Gabála Érenn*, the poet mentions "the Morrigu, daughter of Delbaeth."[67] This line is the source of this epithet, although there are several other places in early Irish texts where the Morrígna are mentioned being the daughters of Delbaeth the father, and Ernmas the mother. Appearing in these geneaologies of the gods, Delbaeth is an ancestor to many of the Túatha Dé Danann deities, and he also appears in *The First Battle of Mag Tuired* fighting alongside the Túatha Dé against the Fir Bolg.[68]

Apart from these brief references, there does not appear to be a narrative literature about Delbaeth. We are essentially left with only his name and relationships with other gods to learn about him. His name is a compound of *delb*, "form, shape, image" or a verbal noun meaning "act of shaping,"[69] and *áed*, "fire." It can be read as "form of fire," "fire-shaper," or variations on this theme. His name could be read more literally as suggesting a kind of creator god who shapes things using fire, like a blacksmith; or more metaphysically in the sense perhaps that his very form is made of fire, he is shaped of fire. Mark Williams points out that he is also related to a "pantheon of skill," a group of gods with powers relating to art and skill such as Ogma, Elatha, Brigid, and the Dagda.[70] Certainly the Túatha Dé Danann as a group and in their stories seem very focused on skill and artistry.

This is the Morrígan's ancestry—a father who is a shaper of fire, and a mother whose name means "iron-death."[71] It is interesting to think about Ernmas and Delbaeth as a couple, the bringing together of iron and fire, which produces among its daughters a trio of war goddesses, weapons forged by that union. One could also contemplate this pairing as a union of deities representing life and death. Considering cosmic or elemental fire as a quickening principle, an embodiment of life force, it's highly poetic that this god is paired with iron-death.

Returning to the *Táin Bó Regamna* encounter between Cú Chulainn and the Morrígan, she changes shape into a bird, and Leahy's translation says, "Then he saw that she had become a black bird upon a branch near to him."[72] *Ba hén-si dub forsin chroíb.* It is worth noting for clarity that the text here isn't referencing the species called blackbird; it is a non-specific bird, *én*,[73] whose color is black, *dub*.[74]

The passage seems to highlight this black color in ways that may be significant, and it's likely that the reader is meant to understand it as a crow or raven. Irish has several ways of saying something is dark or black; *dub* often carries an emotional resonance of ill-fated, gloomy, melancholy, or doomed. This might tend to reinforce the aspect of the story which leads to the place being named Grellach Dolluid, "doomed/ill-fated bog." She also refers to the Brown Bull of Cúailnge as *in Dub*, "the Black one," in the same scene, reinforcing a sense of inexorable doom that surrounds both Cú Chulainn and the bull in this story. Her black form perching on a branch in this scene seems to represent that same sense of doom and is interpreted by Cú Chulainn as a black omen.

Lean, nimble grey-haired hag

In an early Irish text called *The Battle of Magh Rath*, a poem describes an apparition of the Morrígan hovering over the head of one of the kings at this battle:

> *There is over his head shrieking*
> *A lean, nimble hag, hovering*
> *Over the points of their weapons and shields:*
> *She is the grey-haired Morrigu.*[75]

The epithet condenses descriptions from two lines of the poem. The first, in its original Irish is *caillech lom, luath ag leimnig*. The literal meaning of *caillech* is "veiled one," but colloquially usually means an old woman, a nun (i.e. one who has taken the veil), or where there is supernatural context, a witch or hag.[76] *Lomm* is "naked, bare," or with respect to textiles, can mean "thread-bare."[77] *Lúath* is "swift," moving with quickness; translated here as "nimble;" *leimnig* is "leaping, jumping."[78] The other part of the epithet comes from the last line of the verse, *in Morrigu mong-li-ath*: the gray-haired Morrígan. *Mong* is not just hair; it speaks of a long, abundant, untamed mane of hair, and is also used of horses and other "shaggy" natural features.[79]

The poem presents an image of an unabashedly naked witch with a wild mane of gray hair, swiftly leaping through the air over the weapons of the battlefield. Her age and nakedness are emphasized here, in a way that seems calculated to create dissonance. This isn't the only time a naked hag with a wild mane of hair makes an appearance. Badb appears in a similar form in two stories—*The Destruction of Dá Derga's Hostel* and the similar *Da Choca's Hostel*—and both seem to highlight a sort of leering sexuality that is at odds with her frightening, grotesque presence.[80] Images like this seem to present a transgression of social norms about normative female behavior and modesty, and this adds to the threatening quality of her presence.

Devotee Shannon Thompson commented,

This form seems in some ways calculated to instill fear in those on the field… it plays a lot with the deep uneasiness some people feel around a female form that's not at all about the male gaze. Add the nimble movement (which seems like Her enjoyment of Her own physical strength, along with probably being unsettling to watch), the shrieking, the reference to Otherworldly cursing hags elsewhere in the lore, this is a battle horror.[81]

A praise poem about the goddesses of the Túatha Dé Danann in the *Lebor Gabála Érenn*, commonly known as the *Book of Invasions*, has the following:

> *Badb and Macha, great wealth;*
> *the Morrígan, foundation of sorcery:*
> *the guides of savage battle,*
> *the splendid daughters of Ernmas.*[82]

This epithet is from the Irish phrase *fotha felbais*, and its language is poetic and evocative: *fotha* is "foundation, origin, source, or cause;"[83] though alternate manuscript versions of the text have variations in the language here such as *flatha*,[84] which would be "sovereignty, realm, pre-eminence."[85] The second part, *felbais* is "enchantment, sorcery; a charm or spell."[86] It has been translated in a variety of other ways: R. A. S. Macalister has "springs of craftiness," connecting it to the daughters of Ernmas as a group rather than specifically the Morrígan.[87] William Hennessy has "who dispenses confusion," perhaps a reference to the way she uses sorcery to create confusion in adversaries. [88]

She is the foundation of enchantment, the wellspring of sorcery, the Morrígan who dispenses confusion. It speaks to seeing her as the origin from which the learning of sorcery comes.

This epithet is a slightly altered version of a line from the Odras *Dindshenchas* poem, a rich source for so many of our epithets. Gwynn's translated line reads, "The horrid Morrigan out of the cave of Cruachu, her fit abode, came."[89] In the original Irish, that is *in Mórrígan úathmar a h-úaim Chrúachan cubaid.* The description *úathmar* means "horrifying, dreadful, terrifying."[90] It comes from the word *úath*, for "fear, terror," but which in supernatural contexts often means "a horror," a phantom, specter or terrifying spirit.[91] It is both the spirit creature and the feeling that such beings conjure in us. It's this meaning that I've chosen to highlight in the Litany with this epithet.

I am fond of this description of her, in part because I think it holds a mirror up to lingering monotheistic dualism which still influences polytheist thought. A few years ago, the Rathcroghan Visitor Centre (the heritage office which oversees visits to the Cave of Cruachan), began selling shirts with the above quote from Gwynn's translation printed on them. Reactions in the pagan and polytheist communities were quite mixed, with a lot of online commentary to the effect of, "It's disrespectful to call the Morrígan horrid." But in truth, she *is* a horror: an Otherworldly phantom who provokes dread. If we separate this from monotheistic dualism, we can recognize that such beings are part of the spirit ecosystem and are sacred in their own right, and that we don't have to paint beings like her in pretty colors in order to appreciate her. So this epithet reminds me how the Morrígan challenges us to confront things that bring us discomfort.

The second part of the line also tells us that the cave is her home, her proper place: a *a h-úaim Chrúachan*, "her Cave of Crúachan," which is *cubaid*, "fitting, proper, harmonious".[92] It is a place of terrifying Otherworldly creatures: malevolent birds, magical destructive pigs, giant monstrous cats, werewolves—it feels like the poet is highlighting that the Morrígan is kindred to these creatures; she is of a piece with the cave and all its dangerous denizens.[93]

For this epithet from the *Reicne Fothad Canainne* poem, I have used a different translation than the one that is familiar to many people from the work of Kuno Meyer:

> She has come to us from the edge of a pillar,
> 'tis she who has egged us on;
> many are the spoils she washes,
> horrible the hateful laugh she laughs.
> She has flung her mane over her back,
> a stout heart … that hates her…[94]

Meyer's line for this epithet is "horrible the hateful laugh she laughs." His translation uses the word "hate" quite a bit here, creating a picture of an almost evil presence which seems to revel in the speaker's dread, and who "a stout heart" should hate.

I cannot hate her, and this language prompts me to look deeper. The Irish source for the epithet is *dremhan an caisgen tibhe*. Looking at the phrase in detail, *dremhan* is "furious, hasty, vigorous, frantic."[95] *Gen* is a smile or a laugh, and *cais* is an ambiguous term that can refer to either love or hate depending on context.[96] The idiom *caisgen* speaks of something that is at once both bitter and amusing; eDIL calls this "a short, sarcastic laugh."[97] David Greene and Frank O'Connor give "twisted laugh," and Jacqueline Borsje translates this line as "furious the sarcastic laugh she laughs," which is the one I've adopted for this epithet.[98] Rather than hatefulness, what these phrases suggest is a wry, dark sense of humor; a gallows laugh. She tosses her mane over her back, laughing darkly in a moment surrounded by death. I think this will feel familiar to many who have spent time in the company of the Morrígan.

This phrase is found in a text called *Cóir Anmann*, the "Fitness of Names," a medieval treatise on names and their origins, translated by Whitley Stokes. "When Cúchulainn was engaged in that combat with Lóch, there came to him out of the elfmounds the Morrígan, daughter of Ernmas, in an uncouth shape, to check Cúchulainn in the combat."[99] It's another one which could seem disrespectful to some; the English connotation of Stokes' word choice of "uncouth" is unrefined, lacking manners, boorish, uncultured, or even rude. There is a classist feeling about the word.

The Irish material this is translated from is very interesting. The Irish phrase is *richt anaichnidh*. The literal meaning of *anaichnidh* is "unknown, strange, unfamiliar," or even sometimes "unspeakable." The sense here is not so much about social class, and more about being something Other, unrecognizable, alien, and vaguely threatening. Another way to translate this sense in contemporary speech might be "eldritch." This is emphasized by the mention of her coming from the fairy mounds: she represents an intrusion from the Otherworld. This adjective is used to describe her shape, *richt*, a word which speaks of form or shape in the sense of a guise that is put on.[100] The phrase emphasizes that her shape is non-ordinary, alien, and out of place with expected norms, perhaps even a bit transgressive.

The Dagda's wife

In community discussions on the Litany, some expressed discomfort about using an epithet that defines the Morrígan in terms of her relationship to the Dagda and using a word like "wife" that seem to domesticate her or make her power contingent on another's. At the same time, this epithet might invite us to consider how much of this reaction is a projection of contemporary experiences of marriage onto this material. What do the texts actually say about it?

This epithet appears in at a few places. It appears in the *Rennes Dindshenchas* text, in a section dedicated to the ancient monuments of Brú na Bóinne (Newgrange): "The Comb and Casket of the Dagda's wife, i.e. two hills."[101] This line describes two smaller mounds which can still be seen not far from the famous Brú na Bóinne main mound and which are traditionally associated with the Morrígan. Its Irish text is: *Cir 7 Cuirreill mna in Daghda .i. da cnoc. Mna* here is the genitive form of *ben*, "woman."[102] This phrase does mean "the Dagda's wife," but it's also a construction commonly used for "woman of or associated with;" it could also be read as "the Dagda's woman."

The Morrígan and the Dagda are spoken of as a married pair in the *Metrical Dindshenchas*:

Here slept a married pair
after the battle of Mag Tuired yonder,
the great lady and the swart Dagda…[103]

This passage speaks directly of marriage, using the word *lánamain*, a married couple in the legal sense.[104] It also mentions that they stayed together at this place "after the battle of Mag Tuired," a text in which the couple meet for a marital tryst which is framed as something that takes place annually; perhaps suggesting a kind of ritual marriage rather than a more domestic arrangement.

Interestingly, another poem in the same text refers to her as *rígnai ind ríg*, "the king's queen."[105] Gwynn has translated this "the king's consort," but *rígan* is "queen" and the poem here seems to use alliteration to emphasize their matched, equal status.[106] It is also helpful to remember that in myth, marriage among gods speaks about alliance or linking of the powers that each embodies, rather than domestic human concerns like housekeeping, child-rearing and property inheritance. For the Morrígan and the Dagda, one way to think of their marriage is as the union of her protective martial powers and his nourishing powers of hospitality, in the service of sovereignty.

Slippery, black eel

This epithet is drawn from the Leinster version of the *Táin Bó Cúailnge*, and for once, it's been translated pretty directly, without Creative Victorian Intervention. This is one of three forms she assumes to attack Cú Chulainn while he is fighting the warrior Lóch: eel, heifer, and wolf. In this shape she coils herself around his legs, entangling him and causing him to fall in the ford, opening him to attack by Lóch.[107] The text doesn't say much more about why she has chosen this form, but other tales involving eels might offer some insights.

Irish folklore records contain many tales relating to eels. Many of them relate to spooky behaviors attributed to eels, such as the ability to leap out of water to attack people, to grasp their tails in their mouths to form a "wheel" shape and thus travel about on land, to emit strange whistling noises, and to keep secrets about the location of buried treasure.[108]

From the medieval manuscript tradition, another eel story appears in the *Siege of Knocklong*. This she-eel is conjured by a druid to aid in battle, and is monstrously huge with a shaggy mane. Her name is Mongach Maoth Ramhar, which means "long-maned, sleek, thick." She attacks in a similar fashion to the Morrígan: knocking a man down by wrapping coils of her body around him, as well as biting and striking with her tail.[109]

It's interesting to contemplate her choice of taking eel form. Eels are a sort of primordial monster in the natural world. They are ancient, in the sense that their evolutionary form is very old. Some of the larger eel species have a second jaw called the "pharyngeal jaw" which lunges outward to grasp prey and pull it down into the throat, like a Ridley Scott alien—monstrous indeed. Ireland has these as well as the more common Conger and European freshwater eels. It's not made clear which species might have been meant in the description of the Morrígan's form, but it would clearly have been one of the larger ones, which can indeed grow large enough to kill a man.

This epithet brings up a paradox that sits at the heart of the Morrígan's relationship with warriorship, and also with devotees in general. It is based on words she speaks to Cú Chulainn in their encounter in the *Táin Bó Regamna* text, which I edited to make the wording suit for an epithet spoken in third-person.

Leahy's translation gives: "'Thou hast no power against me,' said Cuchulain. 'I have power indeed,' said the woman; 'it is at the guarding of thy death that I am; and I shall be,' said she."[110] The Irish for her line is: *Is oc do ditin do báis-siu atáu-so ocus bia.*[111] This line has been read in a few different ways, from "I am bringing about your death, accomplishing it," to "I am guarding your death-bed," and even "I keep you from death and I will keep you from it."[112] These wildly differing translations hinge on the word *ditin*, which can be read as a form of the verbal noun *díden*, "leading, guiding, or bringing about;" however, it also can be read as a form of *dítiu*, "guarding, sheltering, covering, defending."[113]

There seems to be no consensus on which is the correct way to read this line, and I have often wondered whether it even makes sense to look for a single correct meaning. Irish medieval texts are often multi-layered and use word sounds that would conjure multiple meanings to a listener hearing the stories as oral performance. What if we're meant to hear both? Perhaps the Morrígan is saying to him, "Your death belongs to me and I will bring it to pass in the way I have chosen, and until that time, I protect you." I think this would be compatible with the complexity of their relationship, which is both adversarial and tutelary, and in which he has always known a violent end awaited him as part of his chosen life path.

It has been my observation that whatever this may have meant in medieval Ireland, to contemporary devotees of the Morrígan, this message often comes up in the context of a relationship of guardianship or patronage. I have lost count of the number of times someone has emailed me to say "In a dream, she told me she holds my death, does that mean something?" Many times, this message is received by people who have never heard of the *Táin Bó Regamna*. This tells me that there's something here that is significant to how the Morrígan interacts with her devotees. Perhaps to guard our deaths means she has seen something heroic in us, even when cannot see ourselves in that light.

The wolf is one of the three forms which the Morrígan takes to attack Cú Chulainn during the combats of the *Táin Bó Cúailnge*.[114] This phrase comes from the Leinster version of the *Táin*: "Then the Morrígan came in the guise of a shaggy, russet-coloured she-wolf. While Cú Chulainn was warding her off, Lóch wounded him."[115]

The choice of words is interesting: *riocht saidhi gairbi glasrúaidhi*. The first thing to notice is that *sadh* is not the typical word used for a wolf, either in the medieval texts or in common speech. It is more common to see *faol* or *mac tíre* ("son of the land," a kenning for wolf.) This word *sadh* is a very uncommon word and specifically means "bitch."[116] The First Recension version uses both: *sod meic tíre*, "bitch wolf."[117] These texts are very keen to convey that she is not just any wolf, but a wolf-bitch. She is also described as *garb*, "rough, harsh, rugged,"[118] and *glasrúad* is reddish-gray, or blue-gray mixed with red, like the fur of animals like wolves and foxes often is. There is something that feels quite untamed and primordial about this description.

Of course, Ireland has deep-rooted traditions identifying warriors with wolves or dogs, and in light of this it seems natural for a goddess worshipped by warriors to have a wolf form. The Cave of Crúachan that is her home is also said to be home to wolves. There is a story about three Otherworld women who dwell in the Cave and come out in wolf shape to hunt the land.[119] Wolf beings like these seem to be part of the Morrígan's spirit retinue.

In the *Táin Bó Cúailnge*, on the night before the great final confrontation between the armies of Ulster and Connacht, the Morrígan appears and speaks in the dusk between the two camps:

"It was on that night that the Morrígu daughter of Ernmas came and sowed strife and dissension between the two encampments on either side, and she spoke these words: *Crennait brain…* "[120] This begins a poem in which she seems to warn both sides that their fate in the battle is uncertain. Her actions are described as *indloch*, "cleaving, causing division, slandering, rebuking;" and *etarchossaít*, "complaining of one person to another, stirring up mutual recrimination or strife."[121] The poem ends with "Hail to the men of Ulster! Woe to the Érainn! Woe to the men of Ulster! Hail to the Érainn!" seeming to both warn and bless each side, while inciting them against each other.[122]

It's a curious moment which is sometimes viewed through the lens of the Morrígan as a goddess who simply relishes violence and is sowing strife to incite this violence. We can also consider how she has, from the earliest part of the Ulster tale cycle, been working in the background to bring a long-simmering latent tension to a head in open conflict. There is a sense in which this battle is inevitable, and she is bringing it to the crisis point so that it can be fought and settled.

This vivid image of the war goddess hovering over weapons appears in a poem in *The Battle of Magh Rath*:

> *There is over his head shrieking*
> *A lean, nimble hag, hovering*
> *Over the points of their weapons and shields:*
> *She is the grey-haired Morrigu.*[123]

Her action is *ag leimnig*, "leaping, jumping," over the points of weapons and shields during the battle.[124] This description aligns with many passages in tales of battles in which war goddesses and battle spirits are seen in the air overhead. Sometimes they are called "demons of the air," and often grouped among hosts of frightful, Otherworldly creatures who are drawn to the violence. In a general sense, she is being painted as part of this great mass of spirits over the battle.

But she isn't just hovering over the battlefield—she is leaping over the points of weapons and shields. It might be relevant to think about this line in relation to material that talks about spirits being installed in weapons and shields. This appears in a few texts, but perhaps the most detailed example is the sword Orna which was found in the battle of Mag Tuired. These tales speak about "demons" or spirits which are kept in weapons by means of spells, and who shriek from them and hover over them during combat. These spirits appear to be of the same type as the battlefield spirits who are also seen in the air over battlefields in the company of the war goddesses.[125]

Many are the spoils she washes

This one is from the *Reicne Fothad Canainne* poem once again. The poem dwells quite a bit on images of bloody spoils and entrails, returning to this motif several times:

> *There are around us here and there many spoils whose luck is famous; horrible are the huge entrails which the Morrigan washes. She has come to us from the edge of a pillar, 'tis she who has egged us on; many are the spoils she washes, horrible the hateful laugh she laughs.*[126]

There are two kinds of things being washed by the Morrígan. She washes the spoils, *fodb:* "clothing or equipment taken from the dead," but which can also refer to any valuables seized in conflict.[127] She is also washing the body itself, specifically its entrails, *inathor:* "intestines, bowels, entrails."[128] The entrails on this field are *dímár,* "very great, huge, vast."[129] The battle must have been a great slaughter. Her washing action is *dreman*, "furious, frantic, wild."[130]

The speaker, a dead man whose spirit remains with his body on the battlefield, conveys a deep anxiety that his body lies unwashed in the field. He can see the Morrígan approaching as she furiously washes the carnage and the spoils of the dead, and his spirit begs his lover to gather his spoils and his body and run from the field before she reaches him. It's incredibly evocative and speaks of cultural beliefs about what happens to the spirit of someone whose living relatives don't come to care for their body and possessions after death.

An interesting aspect of this image of the terrifying goddess washing bloody spoils is that it's more familiar as an omen occurring before conflict, in the person of the Washer at the Ford. In this instance it is taking place after—it seems that the arrival of the Morrígan and her washing the spoils of the dead here is very the thing that the omen warns of when seen before battle.

In the first version of this Litany, I published this epithet as "envious queen fierce of mood," which is from Gwynn's translation of the Odras poem in *The Metrical Dindshenchas*. As it turns out, this epithet is a great example of Creative Victorian Translation. The line is: "The envious queen fierce of mood, the cunning raven-caller, brought off with her the bull that lived in miry Liathmuine," which has been translated from the Irish:

Tuc lei tarb in tnuthach,
in rigan garb gnathach,
bai i Liathmuine lathach,
in fiachaire fathach.[131]

Where Gwynn gives us "envious," the adjective is *tnúthach*, "furious, angry; eager for battle;" it can also mean envious, in the sense of greatly desiring something.[132] She is also described as *garb*, "rough, harsh, ungentle," a word also used to describe her in wolf bitch shape; and *gnáthach*, "usual, customary, constant," so she is always this way.[133]

While the Victorian lens conveys a moody, jealous, unpredictable or capricious being, another way to read this might be "the battle-eager one, the queen known for harshness," or "the fierce one, the always-ungentle queen." I have updated this line in the Litany to combine these readings.

Morrígu who brings victory

This epithet appears in one of the lesser-known Irish texts, the *Banshenchus*, or "Lore of Women," an early Irish text about the histories and genealogies of prominent women. It is in a verse text speaking about the great women of the Túatha Dé Danann. "Nemain, Danand, Bodb and Macha, Morrigu who brings victory…"[134] The Irish phrase is *Morrigu nobered buaid*. She is the "bearer" of victory, from the verb *beirid*, which has a broad range of meanings enclosing to carry, to bring forth, to birth, to deliver, to secure or win something.[135] She bears victory, and the word used for this is *búaid*, "victory, triumph," but which also means "gift, virtue."[136]

Búada are not just accomplishments; they are the intangible powerful gifts that mark great persons in myth and saga. In the sagas, these gifts are linked to *geasa*, or ritual prohibitions, which function as magical limitations to circumscribe the power wielded by those who bear heroic gifts. Historian Bernard Mees observes that these likely have a shared origin in initiatory rites: "Geases are also connected in one Irish source with the 'gifts' (*buaida*) enjoyed by some Irish kings and champions, such as Cuchulainn's salmon leap and battle fury. They may have originally been connected with rites undergone by young nobles in early Irish society."[137]

This epithet conveys that it is through the Morrígan that these heroic gifts come to us, and through her that they can bring us to victory in our struggles.

Macha

Macha Red-haired

At the beginning of Macha's series of epithets, this may be the place to introduce the several different incarnations of Macha. She appears as the daughter of Partholon and the wife of Nemed, among the first peoples of Ireland; as Macha Mong-Ruad, queen and founder of the royal site of Emain Macha; as a mysterious Otherworld woman who marries the farmer Cruinn; and as one of the war goddess trio, the daughters of Ernmas. Epithets from each of these groups of stories will appear in her series here.

The epithet "red-haired" is a translation of the name Macha Mong-Ruad, and so it doesn't have a single source, but appears wherever the story of the warrior queen Macha Mong-Ruad is repeated. This includes *The Annals of the Four Masters*, the *Dindsenchas*, the *Lebor Gabála Érenn*, various Ulster tales, the *Banshenchus* or "Lore of Women," and more. This signals how important she is in the story tradition. Mong-Ruad is commonly translated as "red-haired," but *mong* isn't just hair in a general sense, it is a mane of hair, a word often used to describe a horse's mane or the shaggy hair of other animals.[138] It has the sense of length, wildness or of a large volume of hair.

That her mane of red hair is called out in her name signals that this is an important feature of Macha. It hints at her connection to horses, of course. But more than this, it introduces what will be a recurring theme throughout her stories, that of gender. Long and brightly colored hair was felt to be a mark of beauty for women in early Ireland, and a symbol of femininity. That this feature is so strongly highlighted emphasizes her womanhood. This is particularly interesting in light of the story of Macha Mong-Ruad: she is the daughter of a king and stood to inherit leadership, but her male relatives try to deny her on the basis of her gender, so she takes the kingship by right of arms instead. She has to fight for a place as a woman in the male-dominated system of kingship succession. Her name points to a kind of unapologetic femininity which she occupies, refusing to choose between embodying her gender and achieving the authority she has earned.

I also think it's worth saying that I don't think Macha's story needs to be read as reinforcing a cisnormative gender binary. The point of the hair as a symbol is to highlight how boldly she transgresses the gender boundaries of her society. A cheeky way to phrase Macha's message might be, "Gender is performative, bitches, now stand down and give me my crown."

Queen by virtue of her strength

Macha Mong-Ruad's strength is mentioned in several versions of her story in the context of overcoming the sons of her rivals for the kingship. This epithet is adapted from these tellings, such as in *The Annals of the Four Masters*, where it says she "brought the sons of Dithorba with her in fetters to Ulster, by virtue of her strength, and placed them in great servitude, until they should erect the fort of Eamhain…"[139] That is to say, she hunted these rebels down in the wilderness, bound them in fetters using her own strength, and forced them to serve her as laborers, building her royal fortress.

This phrase highlights the fact that she is a uniquely powerful woman. She has already defeated all these men in the traditionally male arena of combat. Now she also demonstrates physical mastery of them through binding them and making them into laborers to support her reign, reinforcing her status as queen.

This epithet comes from the story of Macha the Otherworld woman who married Cruinn, and raced the king's horses while pregnant. It is found in *The Metrical Dindshenchas*, translated by Gwynn: "Then the nimble bright lady bared herself, and loosened the hair about her head: without fierce cry to urge her she came to the race, to the tourney."[140]

Looking at the Irish source text, this starts to look like some Very Creative Translation. "Nimble bright lady" comes from *in mer mend*, where *mend* is "visible, conspicuous," but with respect to a person the sense would usually be more along the lines of "remarkable, notable," or even "powerful."[141] *Mer* is an interesting word, denoting something like a reckless, wild, or demented person, though it can also be used in a more complimentary sense like "spirited, lively, nimble, wild, fierce."[142] It's a very kinetic word, conjuring an image of someone in quick, instinctive motion. Gwynn's "nimble bright lady" translation seems to lean toward a more genteel, demure image, in line with Victorian norms. This could instead be read as "the impetuous, powerful one," or "the notable fierce lady," for example.

This passage comes at the point where the demand that she race the king's horses has been stated, an ordeal which she knows could cause miscarriage or death, but which she must undertake in order to save her husband from execution. There is a sense of recklessness or fearlessness in the face of a terrible, unjust choice. This is enhanced by the description of her loosening her hair (which *is* accurately translated by Gwynn). It's interesting to note that just like with Macha Mong-Ruad, again the hair is highlighted. It's almost as if the reader is meant to begin thinking of her in equine terms here. It's a vivid image. I picture it something like this: Macha gives the king's messengers a hard stare, then lets out a sigh. Then she stands up and gets several heads taller, shakes her hair out of its pins and says "*Fuck it*. Let's go."

Macha, the very shrewd

A *Dindshenchas* poem describes Macha, the wife of Nemed among the first peoples of Ireland, who was a seer. In a visionary dream she saw the destruction to come in the *Táin Bó Cúailnge*, and died of a broken heart. Her death presents the reason for the royal site of Ard Macha to be named after her. Gregory Toner's translation of the poem reads:

> *Very shrewd Macha saw*
> *by means of a vision, graces which we do not mention,*
> *accounts of the conflict of Cooley...*[143]

The phrase is *Macha marglic*, from *glicc*, "shrewd, ingenious, skilled, wise," with an intensive prefix added.[144] The ordinary sense of *glicc* is of great skill, astuteness, and insight; however, it also has a meaning of skill in sorcery or occult knowledge, and it may be this meaning that is intended here, since she is involved in a prophetic act.[145] She is Macha the very shrewd, but also Macha who is great in sorcery, Macha the skilled witch, the far-sighted seeress.

By whose command was the fort of Emain raised

For this epithet, I've paraphrased again from the stories of Macha Mong-Ruad, where she bound the sons of her rival Dithorba into servitude and commanded them to raise the fort of Emain Macha.[146] This story conveys Macha's determination and strength in several ways.

It is said that to lay out the boundary for the fort, Macha took the brooch from her cloak and used the pin to draw a circle around herself, and that became the outline where the rath was built. This is a fascinating image because in its scale it reveals her divinity. Only someone the height of a god could casually touch the circumference of a whole fort with her hand.

I mentioned earlier how Macha placed the sons of her defeated rivals into servitude. After she had captured them, the people of Ulster proposed she have them killed. She refused, however, saying, "it would be the defilement of the righteousness of a sovereign to me."[147] What she means here is that to kill her own relatives would be an act of kin-slaughter, and would de-legitimize the authority that she had fought so hard to establish. So instead, she puts them to labor building the fortress she has marked out. Which both avoids kin-slaughter, and strengthens her position. This is a boss move which not only shames these men, but through making them into manual laborers, strips them of noble rank, thereby denying their line all future claims to kingship. This is part of the significance of the raising of the fort. It is a tangible evidence of her power and queenship.

Fierce for glory

This phrase appears in Gwynn's translation of *The Metrical Dindshenchas*, in the poem about Ard Macha. It is speaking about Macha, the Otherworld wife of Cruinn, who races the king's horses while pregnant.[148]

The Irish phrase is *co ngairge im glóir*. *Co ngairge* is with "roughness, boldness, fierceness."[149] The root of this word *garg* is connected to ideas of fierceness in the sense of prowess, but also roughness and a sort of blunt-spoken or mettlesome nature, perhaps like a tired warrior who feels little patience for social niceties. "Glory" has been translated literally from *glóir*, "brightness, glory, splendour," a loan-word from Latin *gloria*.[150] There is a sense of her showing both an air of boldness and ferocity, and also a bright aura or glow.

I can't help wondering, however, if the author might also have been thinking of *glór*, "voice, sound, noise, loudness."[151] Looking at it this way, the phrase could be "with ferocity in her voice," speaking to the fierce bluntness with which she addresses the men who have unjustly put her in this position. She is on the point of going into labor and she knows just how dangerous this moment is for her; and come the end of the race the harshness of her voice will escalate to a scream that lays a curse on all of them.

Macha is addressed with this epithet in one of the poems in the Roll of Kings section of the *Lebor Gabála Érenn*: "Macha—greatness of pride—head of battle of the Red Branch."[152] The Irish phrase is *Macha méit úalle*. It has been translated fairly directly by Macalister. *Úall* is a lovely word denoting "pride, splendor," used in a poetic sense as the best of something, the pride or flower of that thing.[153] *Mét* is "greatness, magnitude."[154] This phrase is superlative on superlative. She is a magnitude of splendor, the pride of the land.

In the context of Macha's story, I think this epithet offers a reminder of the feminist value of pride. Patriarchal culture discourages pride for women and all those identified with femininity. It reframes women's pride in themselves as vanity. This is a modern lens, but at the same time, early Ireland certainly shared a cultural pressure toward modesty in women. Thus, one of the things Macha's story offers is a reminder that pride can be celebrated and deserved and holy.

There is also an alternate meaning of *úall*, which is "wailing, lamentation."[155] This isn't the common usage of the word, but it does appear in the literature. I can't help feeling that this sense would also apply for Macha. It might be out of place in the context of this praise poem describing the might of Macha Mong-Ruad, but thinking of Macha the wife of Cruinn whose dying wail brings a curse on the men of Ulster, she is truly a greatness of lamentation.

Macha is called Grian in the *Metrical Dindshenchas* poem about the origins of Ard Macha. It is in a passage describing Macha, the Otherworld woman who weds the farmer Cruinn. Gwynn's translation of the passage gives us: "her two names, not seldom heard in the west, were bright Grian and pure Macha. Her father, not without might in his home, was Midir of Bri Leith meic Celtchair; in her roofless dwelling in the west she was Grian, the sun of womankind."[156]

This is pretty fascinating in that it looks like Macha, traditionally a sovereignty and tutelary goddess of Ulster and associated more with horses and territoriality, has been conflated with Grian, a solar goddess. This poem isn't the only place this idea is found; the identification with Grian also appears in the Edinburgh *Dindshenchas,* among other texts.[157] Several details appear here which seem to belong more to Grian than to Macha: she is the daughter of Midir, the *síd* king of Bri Leith; she lives in a "roofless dwelling in the west," which seems to imply the place of the setting sun in the sky. There is a goddess or fairy queen named Grian, whose name means "sun," and she is traditionally paired with Áine, who also has solar attributes. Both are connected with fairy hills in Munster, in the south of Ireland, and interestingly both have some connection with imagery of horses. This material seems to imply a variant mythic tradition, perhaps a regional one, in which Macha and Grian were identified with one another or perhaps were different names for the same goddess.

Setting aside the sun goddesses, this epithet can also be read as poetic metaphor. She is *grian banchuire*, which Gwynn has translated as the "sun of womankind." *Grían* is literally the sun, but it is used poetically as a brightness, a luminary, or as a superlative meaning the best of something, similar to phrases like "the flower of warriorship" or "the pride of Ireland."[158] She is the very best, the pride of womanhood, a shining example.

Swifter than the king's horses

Many sources describe Macha using language like this epithet, as it is a part of the basic narrative of the story of Macha, the Otherworld woman who marries Cruinn and races the king's horses. The specific phrase I've used here comes from *The Metrical Dindshenchas* translated by Gwynn. "Macha daughter of Sainrith mac Inboith came to race the two steeds of king Conchobar at the Fair, after Crunnchu had declared that his wife was swifter than the king's horses."[159] The translation from Irish is fairly direct and doesn't reveal anything new.

Of course, this is an impressive and superhuman feat for any human woman, especially one who is nine months pregnant and ready to give birth, so the fact that she succeeds in outrunning the horses is a marker of her divinity and Otherworldliness. The act of running this race identifies her with horses, especially since some versions of the story describe the twins she gives birth to afterwards as foals.

It's also an act that challenges the martial hierarchy and the king himself. Horses were central to kingship in early Ireland, as well as to the warrior elite in general. All the ceremonies of kingship involve horses or chariot racing, as displays of wealth, power, and martial skill. Thus, the farmer Cruinn's boast is a class challenge against the warrior elite and a challenge to this kingship; this is why the boast merits the threat of a death sentence. Her achievement in winning against the king's horses sends a stark warning: "Your kingship is always contingent on the Otherworld's favor, and you done fucked up when you mistreated this sovereignty goddess disguised as a farmer's wife."

Several sources mention the Macha who was the wife of Nemed, a mythical ancestor to the Túatha Dé Danann and leader of one of the first tribes who are said to have settled Ireland. The story of this Macha is mentioned in various *Dindshenchas* texts, the *Lebor Gabála Érenn*, and the *Banshenchus*.[160] It's in the *LGE* version that this epithet appears: "in the twelfth day after they came into Ireland Macha died, and hers is the first death of the people of Nemed. And from her is Ard Macha named."

There seems to be an emphasis on her being the first of her people to die in Ireland. Hers is not the only one highlighted in this way, and this appears to be a myth motif. Later in the saga when the people of Míl arrive, Donn is the first of them to die in Ireland. His death establishes Tech Duinn, the "House of Donn," the place that the dead go to in the Otherworld.[161] It is as if by being the first of his people to die and be buried in the land, that creates an ancestral link for the people in the land. Macha may be performing a similar function as the first of the people of Nemed to die in Ireland, which is tied to the foundation of Ulster through her burial place.

In highlighting that Macha's is the first death of the people of Nemed, this epithet positions her as a mythic ancestor who forges the link between a people and the land, and who establishes the realm into which they will enter as ancestors after death.

This epithet appears in a poem in the *Lebor Gabála Érenn*, about the mighty women of the Túatha Dé Danann. She is mentioned alongside her sisters, the war goddesses who are all daughters of Ernmas.

Badb and Macha, greatness of wealth,
Morrigu—springs of craftiness,
sources of bitter fighting
were the three daughters of Ernmas.[162]

"Greatness of wealth" has been translated without any great surprises. It is from *met n-indbais*, where *indmas* is wealth, treasure, that which has value; and *mét* denotes magnitude or greatness.[163] Some alternate ways to understand this epithet might include "great treasure," "a plenty of wealth," or "richness in store." All very evocative.

It is worth reflecting on what is actually meant by wealth. Modern people might think of money with a phrase like this. In early Irish society, money as we know it today wasn't in use yet; instead, valuables such as cattle were commonly used as currency. This is a bit different from a money-based society; here the store of value has intrinsic life-sustaining value in and of itself. It's probably relevant that Macha's name literally means "enclosed field," in the sense of a place where cattle were held.[164] In a sense, she is wealth herself. In a livestock-based economy, the land is both the source of wealth and the reservoir that stores it; it is the nourishing fields that grow wealth in the form of cattle.

In the *Metrical Dindshenchas*, in the poem about Ard Macha, a passage speaks about Macha, the wife of Cruinn, who is demanded to come and race the king's horses to prove her husband's boast: "'Arrest ye the chieftain!' said Conchobar, leader in battle, 'till the warrior's fair wife come to a noble race against my steeds.'"[165]

She is *ben bán in balair*. *Bán* is an interesting choice here; Gwyn has translated it as "fair," but it can also have a connotation of blamelessness or purity, emphasizing how she is not deserving of the danger she is in.[166] It can also suggest pallor, as a face that has lost its color, perhaps appropriate for someone facing an ordeal which threatens the lives of her husband, her unborn children, and herself. It's also interesting that Cruinn is being described as a warrior. Elsewhere in the poem, his status as a wealthy farmer and cattle-lord is emphasized, with descriptions like "a man rich in herds, Cruinn son of Agnoman, lord of hundreds." Here, the word used of him is *balar*, an uncommon word that seems to mean something like "chieftain," perhaps intending to emphasize his high status.[167]

The same poem makes clear that Macha the farmer's wife is the same goddess as Macha Mong-Ruad the warrior queen, and Macha the visionary. Whether the poet chooses to emphasize Macha in connection to warriors, chieftains, or cattle-lords, all these associations are part of the makeup of her character.

Noble daughter of redweaponed Aed

For this epithet, the source is the same *Metrical Dindshenchas* poem as the previous one. Here she is identified with her father: "Macha, who diffused all excellences, the noble daughter of red-weaponed Aed, the raven of the raids, was buried here when Rechtaid Red-Wrist slew her."[168] The phrase is *ingen ard Áeda arm-rúaid*. It tells us she is the daughter of Áed, but also that she is *ard*: "noble, lofty, exalted, proud."[169] In a more physical sense, *ard* can also mean "high, tall." It's an evocative description conjuring a proud, imposing figure, the tall, fierce, red-haired daughter of a king named for his reddened weapons.

Áed himself is an interesting figure with a mythic background. Elsewhere his name is usually given as Áed Ruad, "red fire," a name that suggests the red hair Macha inherited from him. He may be the same Áed who is one of the sons of the Dagda. A *Dindshenchas* poem calls him "Aed of the wind-swift horses."[170] The Dagda himself is called by many names and these include Eochaid, "horse-lord," Áed Ruad Ro-fhessa, the "red fire of all knowledge."[171] It's intriguing that not only has Macha inherited red hair from this lineage, but possibly an association with horses as well.

Great with child

This epithet doesn't have a single source; every version of Macha who raced the king's horses mentions her being pregnant. For example, the *Metrical Dindshenchas* poem gives the following passage: "Though their like was not found among the horses of Mag Da Gabra, Cruind, eager and shaggy, said that his wife was swifter, though heavy with child."[172] This is interesting when looking at the original Irish, which reads *a ben balc-thorrach*. The English phrase highlights the burden of being pregnant, but the connotations of the Irish phrase lean more toward strength and power. *Torrach* is "pregnant, swollen," but *balc* is more like "stout, strong, sturdy, powerful."[173] She is his sturdy-pregnant wife, whose strength he is ready to bet his life on. Even while hugely pregnant, she is strong and powerful.

The raven of the raids

For this epithet, I've returned to the *Metrical Dindshenchas* poem that has yielded so many epithets. "Macha, who diffused all excellences, the noble daughter of red-weaponed Aed, the raven of the raids."[174]

It's a memorable and vivid epithet. In the way it's mentioned alongside her being a warlord's daughter, it feels a little like an affectionate nickname that her father might have given her. I like to picture the young Macha going raiding with her father's warbands, perhaps showing some of the ferocity that will eventually lead her to becoming a legendary queen. Impressed with the young girl's spirit, they take to calling her "our little raven of the raids."

The Irish phrase is worth looking at: it is *badb na m-berg*. *Berg* is an archaic word meaning "robbery, plundering, warlike deeds."[175] It's related to the more commonly seen term *díberg*, similarly referring to plunder, raiding, and violence, with a particular connotation of unsanctioned violence, and an association with animalistic "wolfish" behavior.[176] In these encounters she is a *badb*: a word which has a whole constellation of meanings, including "crow," "witch," and of course "war goddess." It reminds me a little of Iron Age Celtic coinage which sometimes shows images of horse-mounted warriors accompanied by a crow or raven in flight. She is the raven of the raids, the witch among the wolf-pack, the daughter of the war-band.

Whose crop is the heads of men that are slaughtered

In a medieval glossary, there is an entry associating Macha with the heads of men that have been slaughtered. It includes a phrase which has been translated as "Macha's harvest," "Macha's mast," or a variety of similar phrases. It's worth looking at the entry in the original Irish. It reads: *Machae .i. badb. nó así an tres morrígan, unde mesrad Machae .i. cendae doine iarna n-airlech.*[177] "Macha, i.e. a crow. One of the three morrigans, from which the mast of Macha, i.e. heads of people that are slaughtered."

The central image for this epithet is *mesrad Machae*, literally "Macha's mast," meaning a harvest of tree-fruits, especially nuts.[178] The glossary takes this image of natural plenty of nutritious nut-crops and equates it with the heads taken from the slaughtered on a battlefield. To the war goddess, it tells us, this slaughter is a rich harvest gathered in. It is both poetic and disturbingly grisly at the same time.

There is an implication that those severing and gathering these heads might be doing so as an offering to her. This image appears again in the story of Macha Mong-Ruad. After she defeats her rivals in battle, it's said that they piled a tribute of heads before her and then went away to hide in the wilderness.[179] In any other story, one might see this as simply a measure of how many of their men had been killed, but here it seems strongly suggestive of an offering, a direct presentation of Macha's mast.

Gentle Macha

This epithet appears in the *Banshenchus*, an early text about the important women of Irish myth and history. It is speaking of Macha, the wife of Nemed, among the ancestors of the Túatha Dé Danann in the time of the first settlement of Ireland. After hearing about Macha the raider and her harvest of severed heads, the sweetness of this epithet is a contrast: "Eva, Cera, laudable Medar, gentle Macha, a lovable company like to assured peaceful rest, were the womenkind of Nemed the strong."[180]

The Irish adjective is *mín*. Its core meaning is something like "smooth;" when used to describe persons, it connotes restraint, courtesy, grace, a smooth-spoken or suave conversationalist.[181] There is a sense of skill within it—gentility less as meekness and more in the sense of a cultivated graciousness. *Mín* also appears in phrases about land, where it means "smooth, level, fertile," which is interesting in view of Macha's name meaning a field for cattle.

Macha's final epithet comes once again from the *Metrical Dindshenchas* poem which has provided such a rich vein of praise. Gwynn's translation of the phrase gives "Macha, who diffused all excellences."[182] The poem addresses all three of the major stories of Macha, but this phrase in particular is describing Macha Mong-Ruad, the warrior queen. It is pretty glorious praise on the face of it, evoking the idea of someone so full of excellence and skill that it radiates from her like an aura.

The Irish source text is *Macha, robráena cach m-búaid*. It's even more evocative than the translation! The verb *robráena* comes from the root *bráen*, "rain, moisture, droplets," so it conveys a sense of blessings raining like life-giving dew.[183] The same verb appears in Irish Christian writings about blessings raining down from the Holy Spirit. In Macha's epithet, the blessings that she rains down are *búaid*, a word which has a rich field of meaning.[184] It is often translated as "victory," but also more broadly means "gift, virtue," especially in an abstract or spiritual sense, as one would talk about the gifts or talents someone might possess. Heroes in the Irish literature are often said to possess *búaid*, and it's these special gifts that bring them victories (and which are tied to the *geasa*, or ritual prohibitions they often must live by.)

This poem is lifting up Macha as a divine source from whom blessings fall like nourishing rain, and who radiates the great spiritual gifts that allow us to become heroic.

Badb

Red Badb

Here at the start of Badb's section of the litany may be the place to mention the meaning of her name. The word *badb* has several meanings in addition to being her name: "crow," especially a hooded crow or scald crow; "witch," or generally a threatening, spectral, or Otherworldly person; and even as a metaphor for "warrior or hero."[185] It is often just by context one can sense which of these meanings is intended. She is all these things and each of them will come up among her epithets.

This particular epithet comes from *Cath Maige Tuired Cunga*, or *The First Battle of Mag Tuired*, from a poem about the scene of battle: "The red Badb will thank them for the battle-combats I look on. Many will be their gnashed bodies in the East after their visit to Mag Tuired."[186] The Irish phrase is *badb derg*. *Derg* is a common color word, and one which has appeared here before, often denoting a vivid or bloody red. Sometimes it is even translated as "bloody," so this phrase could also be translated as "the bloody Badb." Throughout her series, quite a few epithets will attach the color red to Badb, because of her associations with violent death, bloodshed and carnage.

This epithet is an example of that ambiguity that often exists around the word *badb*. It appears in the Leinster version of the *Táin Bó Cúailnge*, where the fighters of Ulster are being mustered to help Cú Chulainn. In a long list of people and places for the messenger to go and seek help, they send "to Úathach Bodba," which has been translated as "the terrible fury" by O'Rahilly.[187] In it, *úathach* is a substantive of "terrible, horrible, dreadful;" and *bodba* is an adjective meaning "deadly, fatal, dangerous, warlike."[188]

If it's read as a proper name, it's "Úathach the deadly;" Úathach is the name of a terrifying female warrior who is supposed to be involved with Cú Chulainn's training. Alternately, it can be "the dangerous terrifying one," or "the warlike horror." It may be relevant that the Morrígan is the very next person mentioned in the list, and some have read this epithet as being a description of her: "go to the terrible fury, to the Morrigan, to Dun-Sobairche…"[189] So while I've placed it in Badb's litany because of its descriptive use of her name, in its original context it can also be read as pointing to a variety of different entities who are adjacent to the war goddesses.

"Fury" is an interesting translation choice here, alluding to entities in Classical literature such as the Greek Furies. While these beings are not themselves part of the Irish mythic landscape, medieval Irish authors frequently did equate them with the Irish war goddesses and the spirits associated with them.

Blue-mouthed, loud-croaking crow

This phrase introduces an image that appears in a few places in the Litany: the war goddess as crow feasting on the dead after a battle. This particular phrase comes from a translation of *Cath Mhuighe Leana*:

> *Red-mouthed, deep-black ravens descended upon the bodies of champions, and upon the carcasses of noble warriors, and upon the broad breasts of combatants, and upon the chests of soldiers; and blue-mouthed, loud-croaking Badbhs rejoiced; and they were all merry and vociferous at the extent of the tables and the abundance of flesh-spoils which they found upon those cold-prostrate men...*[190]

The "loud-croaking" and descending on the bodies to feast evokes carrion birds, but of course the word *badb* is ambiguous so this can also be a proper name, Badb. *Béal-ghorma*, "blue-mouthed" is a less common description than "red-mouthed," a phrase often used to describe blood on the mouths of carrion birds. *Gorm* sometimes means "dark" or even "black" rather than blue per se, or perhaps it could be intended to evoke the iridescent blue sheen that crows can sometimes have.[191] Blue about the mouth of a person, of course, signals death, and there is a kind of double-entendre here that superimposes two images: the carrion birds feasting on the dead, with their blue-black beaks, and a blue-mouthed witch goddess with the look of death about her.

For this epithet I turn to *The Courtship of Ferb*. During a feast, a terrible omen occurs in the form of a sudden, violent blast of wind. This is interpreted as an omen of war, and a poem follows which speaks about the influence of Badb, translated by Rebecca Shercliff:

> *The Badb will destroy; there will be violent strength,*
> *an attack on Medb,*
> *an abundance of slaughter, destruction on a host,*
> *sorrowful the din.*[192]

Elsewhere, Hennessy has translated this line "slaughter upon the host," and this is the line that is in the Litany.[193] It is from Irish *ár for slúag*, where *ár* is "slaughter, carnage, defeat, destruction," and *slúag* is "host, army, company, assembly."[194] It speaks bluntly that this omen warns of Badb, who brings destruction and slaughter to armies. She seems to be both the omen and the destructive force it warns of.

She who darkens the sky with phantoms

I employed a bit of extra poetic license in arranging this particular epithet. It comes out of an early modern Cú Chulainn adventure story called *The Pursuit of Gruaidh Ghriansholus* and is part of a description of a host of battle spirits:

> *Cúchulainn went into the chariot then, and he began his wonderful, numerous, awful feats which were full terrible and frightful. And the sky darkened over him, so numerous were the phantoms and witches and spectres and mad ones of the glen who were shrieking above him, urging him to do battle and combat.*[195]

This recitation of the various Otherworldly creatures in the phantom host is a literary styling that appears again and again in stories in the tradition. For example, here is a similar passage from *Sid na mBan Finn*: "And pale-faced and buck-shaped sprites and red-mouthed battle-demons and the spectres of the glen and the fiends of the air and the giddy phantoms of the firmament shrieked as they waged warfare and strife above the head of the fian-chief wherever he went in the battle."[196] You can see that these passages are drawing on a common poetic trope, and many of them include Badb.

The particular example with the description of phantoms darkening the sky does not directly name Badb, but she is so frequently included in litanies of this group of spirits, that I felt it could just as well describe her. The image of a host of phantoms and specters so numerous they darken the sky is compelling and very evocative of her presence among the spirits of the battlefield.

The source for this epithet is *The Courtship of Ferb*, again. Badb shows up several times to both Ulster and Connacht, to bring warnings to each side, which incite a war by persuading each side that they must attack before they are attacked. The epithet is from a poem verse about a battle which has taken place: "You have feasted the Badb, the pale one, amidst the weapons."[197] She is *Baidb co m-báni*. *Bán* can mean "white, fair, bright," or even "pure, holy, blessed;" however, it can also mean "pale, bloodless," and I think it is this last sense that is intended here.[198] The poem is spoken by Ferb in her grief looking over the dead. The more recent translation of the text by Shercliff agrees, giving "You have fed the pallid Badb."[199] *Bán* also comes up as a verb *bánad*, to go pale with fear, to blanch or be drained of color.[200]

The feeling seems to be of Badb as a ghostly white presence, like an apparition, or the cold, pale skin of the dead. It is a description that evokes the specter of death.

Ferocious of reply

This epithet is found in *The Destruction of Dá Derga's Hostel*. The hag Cailb, who most scholars agree is Badb in disguise, has just given Conaire the prophecy of his destruction, to which he responds, *Is feochair a freagra*. This is translated as "Savage is the reply," by scholar Ralph O'Connor.[201] It is Conaire's commentary on how uncompromising she is; she represents his doom which has come as the result of violating his oaths and obligations as a ruler, and she does not negotiate. He knows he is looking into his imminent death.

Feochair is "stern, severe," and in somewhat later usages, "fierce, indomitable, wild," such as one might say of wild animals, but also of someone who is uncompromising and cannot be deterred.[202] The first version of this Litany used the phrase "savage of reply," as in O'Connor's translation. However, I've changed this since being reminded that "savage" is a common slur used against Indigenous peoples. There are better options to translate this word in a way that won't reinforce that harm, so I've used "ferocious" instead. She is fierce, stern, untamed; she cannot be silenced.

In Cú Chulainn's death tale, he meets three hags who take part in his downfall. The tale exists in two versions, and this epithet is drawn from the earlier version called *Aided Con Culainn*. From Maria Tymoczko's translation: "Before him on the road were three hags of sorcery, blind in their left eyes. They had cooked a lapdog on rowan stakes, with charms and potions."[203] The Irish description of the hags is *ammiti túathchaecha*. An *ammait* is a "witch, hag, woman with supernatural powers;" hence the description that these are sorceresses.[204] *Túathchaech* is an idiom that means evil-eyed, or blind of the left eye; it's literally "left-blind," and has a connotation of supernatural ability to cast the evil eye.[205] These women are full of sorcery, their whole presence is threatening, and they have prepared a trap for him in the form of offering dog meat which will force him into breaking a *geis*.

This tale does not explicitly identify these hags with Badb. They are witches, and the daughters of Calatín, a man slain by Cú Chulainn, and they are seeking to destroy him in retribution. In the Early Modern Irish version of the story, one of the sisters is called "the Badb," however.[206] Their appearance and behaviors are also very characteristic of Badb, so I felt it was appropriate to use their description in the Litany. It's also very similar to a description of a guise used by the Morrígan, as seen earlier.

Fiery red-lipped scald of war

This epithet is found in *Tōgail na Tebe*, a medieval Irish version of Statius's *Thebaid*, a Latin epic about the destruction of Thebes, translated in English by George Calder. It's an interesting example of the medieval Irish habit of using native divinities in place of, or in glosses defining Classical entities. The description is of Tisiphone, a Greek fury who has been conjured and sent to attack Thebes. Her description is very Classical at first: "then the fiendish mad Fury arose with her locks of venomous serpents about her head…" and as she approaches, "horror and vast fear seized them as they beheld the fiendish dusky face of that fiery red-lipped scald of war."[207] It is in this latter passage where Tisiphone has been described using language typical for an Irish war goddess: *na baidbi bruthmaire belldeirgi sin*. She is a *badb*, which as shown earlier can mean a crow, witch, or war goddess, and she is *bruthmar*, "fiery, raging, furious," a word which conveys ardent fury but comes from a literal sense of the heat from fire.[208] She is also *belderg*, "red-mouthed" or "bloody-mouthed," a description that comes very frequently applied to the Badb.[209]

Calder's choice to call her a "scald of war" here is interesting. It is based on the sense of a *badb* as a crow—the Irish scald-crow, or hooded crow. The "scald" in scald-crow is a loan word from old Norse *skald* meaning poet, a role which held as much power as the poets of early Ireland. It's also the origin of the English word "scold." A scald-crow is a poet-crow, a canting crow in whose voice is heard incitement or warning, and who might be the war goddess in bird form delivering prophecy. It seems that the translator is playing on both meanings, leaning into the notion of a war-poetess.

The language that inspired this epithet appears in multiple places, associated with the phenomena of warrior fury. There are several examples in the *Táin Bó Cúailnge* where Cú Chulainn is entering this state: "The torches of the war-goddess, virulent rain-clouds and sparks of blazing fire, were seen in the air over his head with the seething of fierce rage that rose in him."[210] It is part of the transformation that overcomes him when he enters the state known as the *ríastrad*, or "distortion."[211] His body contorts in a monstrous fashion, his hair stands on end like spikes, emanations of heat, smoke, and fire emerge from his head, and a great beam of light called the Hero's Light bursts out of him. Sometimes there is an emanation in the shape of a bird fluttering over him, and sometimes instead of a beam of light there is a fountain of blood. These descriptions center on images of an animalistic state of elevated rage which brings profound, fiery heat.

The Irish phrase appearing in these descriptions is *coinnle bodba* which means "torches or candles of Badb." *Coinneal* is from a Latin loanword, *candela*, and it means candle or torch, and also has a figurative connotation as something which brings light, as one might call a person a "shining light."[212] This phrase is particularly interesting in that it attributes the phenomena of light and heat that burst forth out of the hero to the presence or influence of Badb. She is the blazing spiritual fire that causes this phenomenon of the Hero's Light.

Demon of the air screaming from the rims of shields

In the *Táin Bó Cúailnge*, one of the climactic moments is the fight of Cú Chulainn and Fer Diad, a ferocious battle which has stirred up both combatants to heights of battle-fury, and they are surrounded by agitated spirits. O'Rahilly's translation of the the Leinster recension reads: "Such was the closeness of their encounter that sprites and goblins and spirits of the glen and demons of the air screamed from the rims of their shields and from the hilts of their swords and from the butt-ends of their spears."[213]

This gathering of spirits follows a pattern that appears often in early Irish accounts of battles, where litanies of such creatures are found listed among the frightful phenomena that characterize scenes of war. Often, the lists of creatures include *badba*, or the Badb herself. This particular text presents *boccánaig*, "goat-creatures;" *bánanaig*, "pale specters;" *geniti glinni*, "spectral women of the glen;" and *demna aeóir*, "demons of the air."[214] Some might question the use of the word "demon" as an epithet for Badb, seeing it as a pejorative. It's true that Irish has *deman* as a loanword from church Latin *daemon*, bringing with it the pejorative connotation of an "evil spirit."[215] It's likely that the medieval authors intended us to think of them in these terms. At the same time, before it took on this pejorative sense in Christian usage, the word came in turn from Greek *daimon,* "deity, divine power, lesser god, or spirit."[216] So we could actually say that we are re-appropriating a very old word for spirits who have always been with us but had been rejected by the Church as evil presences. I like to think of Badb joining in solidarity with the kinds of spirits who inspire this kind of institutional fear.

For this epithet, I turn to another of the Classical Latin texts translated into medieval Irish, *In Cath Catharda*, which is a translation of the *Pharsalia* by Lucan, on the Roman civil war. In a scene describing one of Caesar's battles, Lucan tells us of the war goddess Bellona brandishing bloody scourges to incite the fray. The medieval Irish translator has replaced Bellona with Badb: *in Badhbh catha do beith cona sraighlibh fuilidhibh ina laim i timcill na cath ic aslach inn imairicc for na slógaib*; "the war-goddess who is said to be with her bloody scourges in her hand around the battles, inciting the hosts to combat."[217] Stokes gives "the war goddess" but the text here is specific, naming "the Badb of battle." She is said to be *aslach,* "instigating, tempting, inducing" *inn imairicc*, "conflict, battle" on the armies.[218]

It seems that the translator felt their audience would more readily recognize this image of Badb using a scourge to incite the combatants to violence, and so substituted her for Bellona. It's a very visceral image that reinforces the idea of a Badb who instigates and incites combatants to violence.

She whose longing is for fire

In a marginal poem in *The Wasting Sickness of Cú Chulainn* is a vivid depiction of the Badb. A marginal poem is a little verse that the scribe added in the margin of the manuscript, not part of the story itself but perhaps intended as commentary or to illustrate some aspect of the story. The poem reads as follows:

> *Mían mná tethrach atenid*
> *Slaide sethnach iar sodain*
> *Suba luba fo lubaib*
> *Ugail troga dír drogain*

Borsje translates the poem so:

> *The desire of the scaldcrow-woman are her fires*
> *The slaughter of a body thereafter*
> *Juices, body under bodies*
> *Eyes, heads belonging to a raven.*[219]

It's a curious poem that seems to fuse desire in an erotic sense with bloodthirstiness, and it occurs in a text about an encounter with a woman from the Otherworld, so some scholars see it as a warning about liaisons with dangerous supernatural beings.

The first line is the origin of this epithet, and some of the words have glosses added to explain their meanings. *Mná tethrach* has sometimes been translated as "wife of Tethra," but *tethra* can also mean "scaldcrow," and a gloss on the poem clarifies that it is referring to Badb.[220] *Atenid*, "her fires," is also glossed as a kenning for "spear and armor."[221] The poem tells us that what the Badb longs for is spears and armor, expressed as "fires," perhaps thinking of the brightness of light glinting on metal. Or perhaps, since *teine* can also mean a hearth fire and therefore figuratively a home, it could be suggesting that she longs for armaments as they are home to her.[222] At the same time, it suggests that what lies behind this desire is the carnage created by weapons, the bodies and their juices, for she is a crow who feeds on carrion.

This epithet appears in a poem in the verse texts of the *Lebor Gabála Érenn*. Macalister's translation reads:

> *Of the loss of the day of Almon,*
> *contending for the cattle of Bregmag*
> *a red-mouthed sharp-beaked scaldcrow sang*
> *a warning about Fergal's head.*[223]

The Irish phrase for the epithet is *badb bel-derg birach*. This epithet and similar ones appear in a few places in early Irish literature, so that it appears to be a traditional or common way to describe her. Macalister's translation is straightforward enough, "sharp-beaked, red-mouthed scald crow," but one could equally translate this as "sharp-tongued, red-mouthed witch." *Birach* is "sharp, pointed," when said of someone speaking, it has the sense of "sharp-tongued," but it also applies to animals in the sense of having claws, beaks, and horns.[224]

It's also worth remembering the social connotations of someone who is *birach*; the word appears in legal texts describing individuals practicing unsanctioned satire poetry: "In *Bretha Crólige* the *birach bríathar* (lit. 'one who is sharp with words') is classed along with the female werewolf and the vagrant woman."[225] The passage highlights the fear with which uncontrolled magical speech was held—the words of such a woman could be as dangerous as the teeth of a ravening werewolf. There is a sense that Badb, who is singing a poem of warning in this epithet, is just such a dangerous, sharp-tongued poet.

In *The Destruction of Dá Derga's Hostel*, the hag Cailb appears on the doorstep of the house where the king is, and most scholars interpret her as Badb in disguise. She curses him, chanting a litany of her names. The entire list of names merits study in itself, but here I have chosen the curious epithet, Mede. Ralph O'Connor translates this as "headless one."[226] More generally, *méide* is "lower part of the neck... nearly always used of the neck of a decapitated body," appearing in idioms to refer to a headless person.[227]

This is a strange and fascinating name for this war goddess to call herself, no? It seems to be part of a recurring theme in this particular text associating Badb and other *síd* people with sacrifice. In another section of the tale, observers describe the "Room of the Badbs," but the occupants of that room are described as if victims of sacrifice:

> I saw three naked ones on the ridge-pole of the house, gushes of their blood coming through them, and the ropes of their slaughter around their necks.
> I know those, he said, three chosen ernbaid. Those are the three who are destroyed every time.[228]

I will return to these three strange, bloody figures associated with her, in a later epithet. For now, just notice that these allusions associating her with violent death are in the background of the tale when she appears in this posture of malevolent warning and calls herself "headless one." In this epithet, she seems to identify herself with the dead, and not for the first time.

This epithet appears in the Boyhood Deeds of Cú Chulainn, which is an episode in the *Táin Bó Cúailnge* in which Fergus relates a long series of tales about Cú as a child. In this tale, the young Cú is asked to go and find his wounded foster-father Conchobor, and to bring him back from the battlefield. Cú sets out and finds that the battlefield is now haunted by horrors and revenant dead people. O'Rahilly's translation from the First Recension reads:

> *He went on his way then. The night was dark. He made for the battlefield. He saw in front of him a man with half a head carrying the half of another man on his back... They wrestled then and Cú Chulainn was thrown. He heard the war- goddess crying from among the corpses. "Poor stuff to make a warrior is he who is overthrown by phantoms!" Whereupon Cú Chulainn rose to his feet, and, striking off his opponent's head with his hurley, he began to drive the head like a ball before him across the plain.*[229]

It is a compelling image of the Badb as a voice crying out on the battlefield, perhaps grieving with the dead, and then challenging little Cú to incite him to rise up and overcome the phantoms.

However, it gets even more interesting when looking at the Irish text, which actually does not speak of crying at all. It says, *Co cuala ní, in mboidb dinib collaib.* In its characteristically terse prose, this is "Behind him, the Badb among the corpses." She is simply looming behind him among the dead. The author has employed a wonderfully creepy idiom to say she is behind him, however: *co cuala ní,* literally, "at the back of his neck."[230] This vivid phrase conjures a terrifying moment for young Cú Chulainn, where he is already being menaced by half-dismembered walking dead men, and then suddenly he hears the voice of the war goddess *right at the back of his neck* harassing him. A cinematic ghost story jump-scare. The night is indeed dark and full of terrors.

Returning to *The Destruction of Dá Derga's Hostel*, the descriptive elements making up this epithet appear within a description of Cailb's arrival at the hostel where the king is staying:

> *When they were there they saw a lone woman coming to the door of the Hostel, after sunset, and seeking to be let in. As long as a weaver's beam was each of her two shins, and they were as dark as the back of a stag-beetle. A greyish, wooly mantle she wore. Her lower hair used to reach as far as her knee. Her lips were on one side of her head.*

She came and put one of her shoulders against the door-post of the house, casting the evil eye on the king and the youths who surrounded him in the Hostel.[231]

Her description is intentionally grotesque, but in this epithet I have chosen to highlight the particular aspects that relate particularly to why she is there: she is alone, and casting evil eye. In the context of the story, her appearing in this way, alone on the threshold, signals to Conaire and his men that they are doomed. His *gessi* (ritual prohibitions) prohibit him from receiving a solitary woman after sunset; but likewise, it is also prohibited for him as a king to deny hospitality to her. It is a trap, and he is doomed no matter his choice.

Even before she says a word, her presence on the threshold signals this threat, both because she is a lone woman after sunset, and because she has the evil eye in her glance. The word used to describe her glance is *admilliud*, "the act of completely destroying; destruction, ruin… blighting," a word also used to describe injury by magic, such as through the evil eye.[232] She looms on the threshold, bringing utter destruction with a silent glance. And then she begins to speak…

Bitch

This scene with Cailb at the threshold of Dá Derga's Hostel is also the source for this next epithet. It is among the list of names Cailb sings when asked to identify herself:

> *"Lo, many and numerous are my other names," she said.*
> *"What are those?" said Conaire.*
> *"Not difficult," she said.*
> *"Samain, Sinand, Seiscleand, Sodb, Saiglend, Samlocht…"²³³*

The list of names continues, but the one I've chosen here is *sodb*, a she-wolf or wolf bitch.²³⁴ This word has come up in the Litany before: when the Morrígan takes on wolf shape, the same word is used to describe her form. It is an uncommon word and not the typical way to say "wolf" in Irish—this text really wants us to know she is a bitch wolf. This is interesting in part because it's the only place I'm aware of where Badb is associated with wolf shape, something that is more commonly attributed to her sister the Morrígan.

For the Litany, I chose to include this epithet simply as "bitch," because I like that it leans into the contemporary sense of the word as a woman who gives no fucks, who does not soften or justify herself. She is here to terrify and to destroy.

Fire of judgment

This epithet is a little different from most in the Litany. Rather than describing Badb herself, in its original context it describes the effect of her presence. It is found in a poem describing the hero Loegaire, in *Bricriu's Feast*:

> *A fury of war, a fire of judgment,*
> *A flame of vengeance; in mien a hero,*
> *In face a champion, in heart a dragon…[235]*

That first line uses language that is often seen describing the Hero's Light with its fiery phenomena like the Torches of the Badb, seemingly a manifestation of her. The Irish phrase is *barc bodbae bruth brátha*. John T. Koch and John Carey translate *barc bodbae* as "fury of war," but one could also read this as "vessel of Badb," or "Badb's hero." *Bodbae* is the genitive of her name, and can mean "deadly," "of/pertaining to war," or "of/pertaining to Badb."[236] Translated literally, *bárc* means vessel, in the sense of a ship or boat, but it's also used poetically to refer to a prince or warrior.[237] There is a sense in this poem that the hero is a vessel possessed by the indwelling presence of Badb, a presence which emerges as heat and fire. "Fire of judgment" has been translated fairly literally from *bruth*, "heat, blaze, fury, vehemence;" and *brátha*, judgment as in legal precedent, also doom or destruction.[238]

It might feel provocative to praise Badb as a "fire of judgment." Judgment is an edged weapon, in a way. Combined with violence it can be a truly dangerous force in humanity, and not one to be celebrated. In a society that seeks to be inclusive of differences, we may be asked not to be judgmental toward others. At the same time, practicing judgment, in the sense of discernment, is what allows us to set healthy boundaries, and to identify and fight injustice. For me, an important thing to consider is that the "fire of judgment" that he's inspired by in this reading of the poem is the presence of the goddess herself, not his own rage. In a justice-oriented approach to this material, the warrior class should be acting in the service of a greater collective, inspired by this goddess but working within a framework in which warriors are accountable to their society's judges or wisdom-holders, not just their own violent impulses. For me, one of the interesting aspects of this epithet is that it can remind us both of what is best in a warrior tradition, as well as the dangers it can present when misdirected.

For this epithet, I turned to *Dá Choca's Hostel*, a story that strongly parallels *The Destruction of Dá Derga's Hostel* as a story about a king breaking his *gessi* and coming to his death as a result. Along the way, Badb appears in the form of the Washer at the Ford: "As they were there they saw a red woman on the edge of the ford, washing her chariot and its cushions and its harness. When she lowered her hand, the bed of the river became red with gore and with blood. But when she raised her hand over the river's edge, not a drop therein but was lifted on high; so that they went dryfoot over the bed of the river."[239]

This entraps Cormac into breaking another *geis*, as he is prohibited from crossing with dry feet over a river. She then delivers a prophecy of his destruction: "And then, standing on one foot, and with one eye closed, she chanted to them, saying: 'I wash the harness of a king who will perish' etc." Just like in *The Destruction of Dá Derga's Hostel*, it's a sequence of bad decisions that build on each other until he is trapped by his fate. These stories highlight Badb as the agent of the Otherworld's retribution for misuse of power.

This is the description given of her: *A mbatar ann confacatar mnái ndeirc for ur ind atha, 7 si ag nige a fonnad 7 a fortche 7 a fodbae*. She is a "red woman," *mnái ndeirc*, a color indicating bright, bloody, or even gory red.[240] She is engaged in washing the *fonnad*, wheel-rims, *fortche*, rugs or cushions, and *fodbae*, general spoils or equipment, of a chariot.[241] This in itself is interesting because most stories that present a Washer at the Ford have the blood being washed from the personal effects—clothing and armor—of the one who is doomed. Here, it's very specifically the chariot and they've not just mentioned the chariot, but have described its different pieces of bloodied equipment. This sends a few visceral messages. For one, the chariot is a symbol of kingship and is used in coronation rites, so her action conveys not just that he will die in battle but that his authority has been destroyed. Also, it suggests a degree of shocking brutality to the death he is being warned of: imagine the level of violence that would result in soaking all the chariot equipment even to the wheel-rims in his blood.

This story is clearly intended to shock and it can be unsettling for devotees to think about. Folks may find themselves wondering, will I face this kind of wrath if I can't fulfill a vow or a commitment in my own devotional practice? I think it's valuable to remember that this is not just about breaking commitments; this is someone who has violated oaths of office for the most powerful position in the land. While we should always take our commitments seriously and do our best to fulfill them, I don't think stories like this should make us live in fear of our beloved goddess. What it does convey is just how deadly seriously she views abuse of power.

I touched on this epithet earlier in the discussion on "headless one." It comes from the *Destruction of Dá Derga's Hostel*, in the passage titled The Room of the Badbs:

> *I saw three naked ones on the ridge-pole of the house, gushes of their blood coming through them, and the ropes of their slaughter around their necks.*
> *I know those, he said, three chosen ernbaid. Those are the three who are destroyed every time.*[242]

The word used to describe the occupants of the room, *ernbaid*, is treated as obscure by both O'Connor and Stokes, and left untranslated. O'Connor quotes a scholar who suggests it may be a corruption of *erbaid*, "destruction." It is actually a recognizable compound word that means "iron-death," from *iarn* "iron," and *bás*, "death," and appears in quite a few other places.[243] The name Ernmas, the mother of the Morrígan and her sisters, is also a form of this same word.

Here are these *tri ernbaid úagboid*, "three chosen iron-dead" or "three chosen for iron-death," three dead individuals still seen with the blood and ropes of their slaughter upon them, and seemingly identified with Badb in some way. It is not clear whether the "ropes of their slaughter" refers to literal ropes used to garrote or hang them, or may be a kenning for entrails.

O'Connor comments on the sacrificial imagery:

> *...it is hard to avoid thinking of sacrifice: the references to blood and to ropes around necks recall the ways in which early Christian writers elsewhere in Europe represented heathen sacrifices. In the Old Norse poem Havamal, which may date from the twelfth century in its extant form, the god of war Odinn reports that he sacrificed himself to himself by being hanged on the world-tree and stabbed with a spear. A Carolingian commentary on the classical Roman author Lucan likewise alludes to men being sacrificed to the Gaulish god Esus by being hanged on a tree and then stabbed.*[244]

Garroting combined with throat-cutting was an attested Iron Age sacrificial practice as evidenced in some of the bog bodies such as Lindow Man, and it's possible that this is what is described here.[245] Perhaps this is shown as an omen for what awaits Conaire, a king who has violated his oaths.

Here is another amusing instance of Creative Victorian Translation. The epithet comes from a poem about a battle in *The Tale of Mac Da Thó's Pig*:

> *There came conquering Conchobar,*
> *Ailill of the hosts, and Cet;*
> *The brooding scald crow was met,*
> *No law Cú Chulainn granted.*[246]

It seems to be saying that on the battlefield, ominously brooding crows met these men. It gets a bit more interesting looking at the Irish source material for the line referring to the scald crow: *bodb iar n-araib for a slicht.* It tells us that Badb, or the scald crow, is "after slaughter," *áraib.*[247] This seems to be meant not in the temporal sense of "afterward," but rather in the spatial sense of "following after," because it continues with the phrase *for a slicht,* "on the track of."[248] This is a much more visceral description, conjuring the scald crow sensing slaughter and following the track of these armies to seek it. One could also translate it, "the scald crow following the track of slaughter." It is more a sense of carnivorous seeking than of dark mood. It also describes the natural behavior of carrion birds who would be aware of the activity of armies, and learn to follow them in anticipation of the feast to come.

Ravenous, red-clawed carrion

This phrase appears in a late (for the Irish tradition) Cú Chulainn story from the 17th century, called *The Pursuit of Gruaidh Ghriansholus*. It's a wild adventure tale, and this epithet comes from a description of the various phantoms and battle spirits that surround Cú Chulainn. "Then it was that there assembled, around Cúchulainn and Garuidh, that band which was wont to accompany Cúchulainn, to wit war-goddesses and sprites and ravenous, red-clawed carrions, for they were wont to get their sustenance from the hands of Cúchulainn."[249]

The collection of spirits here include *bádhbha*, war goddesses, witches or crows; *bocánaigh*, goblins or horned spirits; and *caróin chíocracha chrobhdhearga*, which is the source of this epithet. The language here is idiosyncratic: *carón* is an uncommon word that seems out of context here or may have been misspelled. O'Rahilly seems to have taken it as a loan-word from English "carrion," presumably meaning carrion bird. If this was the author's intention, it suggests that the *bádhbha* alongside them are not just crows, but war goddesses, as they've been mentioned separately from the carrion-birds. These "carrions" are *cíocrach*, "ravenous, greedy,"[250] and *crobhdhearga*, red or bloody of claw, suggesting that they have already been tearing at flesh.[251]

The *crobhdhearga* suggests a connection with an Irish folk saint known in southern Ireland around the Paps of Anu mountains in County Kerry. There, a Saint Crobh Dearg has a tradition in the area, being venerated at the holy well at a stone fort which bears her name, Cathair Crobh Dearg, "Fort of the Red-Handed" or "Fort of the Red Claw." She is said to be one of three sister saints beloved in the area.[252] These saints lack formal hagiographies and are mostly known from folk tradition, but some scholars and archaeologists studying the area have speculated that they could be a folk survival of the war goddess triad.

There is an ambiguity that sometimes appears in the source texts about the identities of Badb and the Morrígan, and it is reflected in this epithet. The phrase comes from *The Second Battle of Mag Tuired*. After the battle, the Morrígan appears and gives two prophecies about what is to come, and this act of prophecy is introduced by saying, "Then after the battle was won and the slaughter had been cleaned away, the Morrígan, the daughter of Ernmas, proceeded to announce the battle and the great victory which had occurred there... And that is the reason Badb still relates great deeds."[253] The text here seems to casually equate the Morrígan and Badb as if they are one and the same. It is an example of how even in the early sources, there seems to have been a diversity of views on how these goddesses relate to each other. It may help to recall that "the Morrígan" is a title more so than a name, and that this passage can also be read as, "the Great Queen, the daughter of Ernmas, proceeded to announce the battle and the great victory which had occurred there... And that is the reason Badb still relates great deeds."

This passage emphasizes the role of Badb as a poet and seer. She is announcing the news of the battle and the history-making deeds that had been done to the whole of the land, "to the royal heights of Ireland and to its *síd*-hosts, to its chief waters and to its rivermouths." The establishment of the sovereignty by the Túatha Dé Danann and the overthrow of the Fomoire is being conveyed across the land, and it is her role to do so. With this comes also the speaking of prophecies for what this change will bring to the land. Not only does Badb perform this in the moment, the text suggests that it is perpetually her role, from ancient times to the writer's present moment, she "still relates great deeds." There is a sense of her as historian—an observer who is present throughout time as events unfold and transmits them to posterity in poetry. Perhaps it is her timeless, Otherworld perspective that also positions her to access visionary knowledge of what is to come.

In this epithet, it is the voice of Fer Diad speaking, the fos-
ter-brother and lover of Cú Chulainn, from the *Táin Bó Cúailnge*. It is at the point in the story where they both know they
must fight one another, and that this will inevitably bring death
to at least one of them. As he is readying himself to meet Cú in
combat, Fer Diad seems to be talking himself into facing this terrible fate: "Let us go to this encounter, to contend with this man,
until we reach that ford above which the war-goddess will shriek.
Let us go to meet Cú Chulainn, to wound his slender body, so
that a spear-point may pierce him and he may die thereof."[254] It
is quite a sad moment that highlights the ways in which the *Táin*
mirrors classical tragedy.

Looking at the Irish from which this has been translated, the
First Recension text has *áth forscara in badb*. Interestingly, the
verb *scaraid* doesn't suggest vocalization; it speaks to action, with
meanings of "overthrow, sever, attack, destroy, separate."[255] The
Leinster version of the text has *áth fors ngéra* in *Badb*, which is
closer to how it's been translated, with the verb *gairid*, meaning
"cry, call out, invoke, summon."[256] O'Rahilly seems to have used
the meaning conveyed in the Leinster version of the poem in
both translations. Later translations by Thomas Kinsella and Ciaran Carson use this same meaning as well.[257]

What does it mean that the Badb will shriek over the ford?
Fer Diad seems to be speaking to his sense of doom. Where the
Táin and other Ulster tales speak about hearing the shrieking of
the war goddesses, it often marks death. Badb and Bé Néit and
Némain shriek over the camps of the warriors, causing a hundred
of them to fall dead of terror.[258] Or war goddesses and battle
spirits are heard shrieking over the field, inciting the violence,
and prophesying who will die. His poem conveys the feeling of
tragic inevitability, that whatever happens in their encounter, the
Badb's voice will be heard for someone's death.

Considering the First Recension version, the emphasis shifts.
It might be translated something like "the ford upon which Badb
will attack/destroy." The sense of doom and inevitability are still

here but there is a heightened feeling of fear here, too. Not only is one of them doomed to die, now he seems to be imagining that destruction being visited by the war goddess herself. Perhaps Fer Diad is struggling here with the knowledge that Cú Chulainn is a favorite of the war goddess and so he may have to face the might of both of them, making his own death that much more certain.

Beyond Fer Diad's anxieties, these poems build a picture of the Badb as a terrifying presence who seems drawn to this fateful encounter, whose voice might be heard inciting the violence, crying out someone's doom, or who might herself join the attack.

Continuing some of the themes from the last epithet, this one speaks to the idea of the prophetic voice of the war goddess. It comes from a poem in the early modern tale *The Pursuit of Gruaidh Ghriansholus*. Cú Chulainn's charioteer Laoi is encouraging him to be ready for a battle. O'Rahilly's translation reads:

> Carrions shall be voracious
> when they see the wounds [dealt by thee],
> and the cries of vultures shall foretell
> the [shedding of] blood.[259]

The word translated here as "vultures" is *badhbha* (which has also appeared in previous sections in its older spelling of *badba*), meaning crows, war goddesses, or spirits of battle. It isn't clear which of these meanings is intended here. The verse has mentioned carrion birds growing voracious and excited at the sight of wounds, so this could imply that the emphasis here is on crows who are drawn to battlefields to feed on the bodies. The sense of prophecy could suggest that these aren't just ordinary corvids, however, but spirits of the battlefield who have the power to foretell whose blood it is that will be spilled that day.

One might also be reminded of the intelligence of corvids, who can learn to anticipate where bloodshed might occur from observing the movements and behaviors of troops. They might gather in advance of conflict and be heard making noise around the area, giving voice to the gathering tension. This can be seen as a kind of prophecy in itself.

In *The Battle of Allen*, a poem describes the scene of the battle:

At midday in Allen
contending for the kine of Bregia,
the red-mouthed, javelin-armed Badb uttered
a paean round Fergal's head.[260]

Where Stokes has translated "javelin-armed," the phrase is *Badb belderg birach*. I've touched on *belderg*, "red-mouthed" in an earlier section. *Birach* is "sharp, pointed."[261] It's a word often used to mean sharp-tongued, and particularly in a phrase along with "red-mouthed" this is probably more the intended meaning, but it can also refer to sharpness in objects such as weapons, or the sharp beaks or horns of animals.

Stokes has embroidered this a bit to paint an image of her armed with a javelin. He seems very pleased with himself about it, too, as he uses this translation for *birach* twice in this text. He gives "Thankful was the javelin-armed foul-mouthed Badb that hour, and sad were the loving mothers, wailing and lamenting and keening for the noble children." The Irish phrase here is *Badb birach belsalach*. Here, *belsalach* is "dirty mouth," which has been translated literally. This word could also be taken as "vicious-mouthed," referring to harsh words, which is probably more in line with what was meant and underlines the sense of *birach* as "sharp-tongued."

It's a very colorful phrase: Badb with the sharp, cursing mouth. Thinking about it this way, there can be a bit of a double-entendre: cursing as in foul language, swearing; and cursing as in speaking magical curses, or swearing doom on someone. I'm not sure if the early Irish had tender sensibilities about words or would recognize the idea of swear-words in the way that we do, but they certainly had strong norms about who was allowed to invoke curses and under what circumstances. In this sense, it's very in character for Badb to be associated with the intentional transgression of social norms to shock and disturb.

White lady

This description appears in *The Courtship of Ferb*. Badb makes appearances to both Ulster and Connacht sovereigns, egging them on to go to war with each other. In this text, Badb appears in a guise that is fair-haired, bright, and wearing signifiers of wealth and rank: "he saw a beautiful woman coming towards him [as he lay] in his bed. She had a queenly appearance. She had curly, wavy, yellow hair [tied up] in a hair-band around her head. Borders of silk were next to her fair skin. There was a soft, smooth scarf of green silk around her neck. There were two round-toed sandals of white bronze between her soft feet and the ground."[262] While the text mentions fair skin, I strongly believe that modern concepts of race do not apply to the gods and so it's important to avoid reading whiteness as a racial concept into this description. The focus is much more on her bright, shining aspect and the beauty of her attire.

The epithet itself is spoken by Medb on acknowledging her presence: "O white lady, fair with brilliancy." Here again the focus is on light and beauty. The line is *a bé bán bulid co llí*[263]. *Bán* means "white, fair, bright," but can also have the connotation of "pale, bloodless."[264] Leahy has translated *builid* as fair, which should be read in the sense of "beautiful."[265] She is beautiful with *lí*, that is "lustre, glory," still emphasizing the general sense of brightness, although this word also can appear in phrases indicating loss of color and bloodlessness.[266] Shercliff translates this line as "O fair woman, beautiful with splendour."

The emphasis in these descriptions is on beauty, brightness and brilliance, along with shining, colorful, and wealthy clothing. The poetry conveys a sense of an Otherworldly glow and radiance. At the same time, there is a suggestion of pallor and bloodlessness too. Medb responds to Badb's warning, asking "what dreadful tale are you telling?"[267] The adjective here is *úathmar*, which is "horrific," specifically in the sense relating to spectral horrors and ghosts. So Badb is bright and shines, but her ghostly color also underlines the horror of the message she brings.

This spectral aspect becomes prominent later in the story after there has been fighting and she is among the dead on the battlefield. Her paleness here takes on another meaning: "You have fed the pallid Badb by means of battle-equipment."[268] The phrase here uses the same word *bán* once again, but here its context points to pallor as of the face drained of color in death. The paleness of her coloring seems to take on a more dreadful aspect as the tale progresses. The liminality of a being who at once embodies shining Otherworldly radiance and the ghostly pale aspect of the dead at the same time, seems entirely appropriate for Badb.

Badb who shall destroy

This final epithet for Badb also comes from *The Courtship of Ferb*. During a feast, a terrible omen appears and the druid interprets the omen in poetry, including this verse:

The Badb will destroy; there will be violent strength,
an attack on Medb,
an abundance of slaughter, destruction on a host,
sorrowful the din.[269]

The verb here is *brisfid*, "break, smash; destroy."[270] What I find intriguing is that the violent strength which will be shown, the attack against Medb in which there will be slaughter and destruction of hosts—these phrases describe the action of the armies of Ulster and Connacht. Yet all this violence and destruction is ascribed to Badb. In the same story, she was shown indirectly causing the war by warning each side that they must attack lest they be attacked.

Here, it seems that the violence on the field itself is framed as her destruction, as if she embodies everything that takes place on the field of battle. There seems to be a hint of something mythic here, too. It does not say what Badb will destroy; there is no target. It is almost a statement of cosmology. Destruction will come as inevitably as creation, worlds end and begin again. Badb will destroy.

Némain

In beginning the series of epithets for Némain, this may be the place to touch on the meaning of her name. There's a lot of confusion in the literature about her; which is perhaps suitable to her character as a goddess who brings confusion. Some sources give a meaning of "battle-fury, frenzy, strife," or even "murder."[271] However, it appears to me that these meanings are derivative of her character, because the etymological roots of the name don't carry these meanings. Some etymologies trace the name to *neim*, "poison, venom," or in a more general sense, "malefic power."[272] Another etymology traces her name to *nem* which means "sky, heaven" and appears in words like *nemed*, pertaining to sacredness or that which is set apart for the holy, such as a sanctuary.[273]

I will not try to resolve these different theories of her name here. Each of these threads will continue through the commentaries on the epithets to come. I also think it's interesting to notice the contrasts between the semantic field containing "frenzy, fury, strife," and that containing "heaven, sanctuary, sacredness." They are almost opposites: the noise and chaos of battle, and the still holiness of the sanctuary. All of these meanings seem appropriate for a war goddess: frenzy and violence and the malefic, dangerous power that stirs it up, and which would perhaps be seen to hover with the crows and ravens in the heavens overhead.

Némain and her husband, the war god Néit, are called "venomous" in a medieval Irish glossary, the *Sanas Chormaic*. The entry is glossing the name Beneid, "wife of war," including the following comment in mixed Latin and medieval Irish: *Beneid .i. neid nomen viri. Be uxor ejus nemon a ben ba neimneach tra in lanamainsin.* "Beneid, i.e. Neid his name. Nemon his wife. A venomous couple truly, was this."[274] This is a play on the folk etymology tracing her name from *neim*, "poison," where the author has emphasized this by also calling the couple *neimneach,* "venomous."

It's worth noting that while modern English distinguishes things like venom, poison, and toxin as different things, early Irish dealt with these ideas more poetically. "Venomous" here doesn't necessarily refer in any specific way to animal venom or plant poison. In fact, *neimnech* as applied to persons or their behavior also has more general meanings of "deadly, dangerous, vindictive, or intense."[275] They are a malefic, dangerous, deadly couple, who bring war.

Wife of war

This epithet appears in a few different places, not just from a single translation. It is a name or title of a war goddess who appears in the *Táin Bó Cúailnge* and a few other early Irish texts.[276] It's a tricky title to parse. Depending how you read it, it can mean "woman of war," "wife of war," or "Néit's wife." *Bé* is "woman," which can also mean "wife" in a genitive phrase.[277] *Néit* means "war" generically, and appears in many phrases pertaining to warfare, but is also the name of the god Néit.

When this title appears in the texts, it's not always clear who Bé Néit is describing—it seems to be applied to more than one of the war goddesses. Most instances of its use pertain to either Némain or Badb, although there is one source (in the First Recension of the *Táin*) where Badb, Bé Néit, and Némain are mentioned together; here it's not clear who the title indicates, but it could be the Morrígan. But most often it's Némain who is paired with Néit, and it's this couple who have a body of *Dindshenchas* lore about the fortress they lived in together at Ailech Néit (the site of what is now the Grianán of Aileach in County Donegal.)

Figuratively, the epithet "wife of war" suggests a bringer of battle, a midwife of destruction, one who is intimate with and intimately bound to the primal force of violence. Thinking of her as frenzy, fear, or danger, she is a wife of war in the sense that these forces are present wherever battle takes place.

In this epithet, the focus centers on an important feature of Némain: her terrifying voice. The source for the phrase is in the *Táin*, the Book of Leinster version. In response to a heroic shout from Cú Chulainn, she appears among a host of frightening creatures: "And the goblins and sprites and spectres of the glen and demons of the air gave answer for terror of the shout that he had uttered, and Nemain, the war goddess, brought confusion on the host. The four provinces of Ireland made a clangour of arms around the points of their own spears and weapons, and a hundred warriors of them fell dead that night of terror and fright in the middle of the encampment."[278] The First Recension version reads, "That night Badb and Bé Néit and Némain shrieked above them at Gáirech and Irgáirech so that a hundred of their warriors fell dead of fright. That was not the most peaceful night for them."[279] There are a few more examples that are fairly similar to this. Sometimes it's implied that it's the noise and chaos of the army itself that causes them to die of fright, but she instigates that chaos. Other times it's her shrieking voice directly causing the terror.

The place names mentioned above, "Gáirech and Irgáirech," are evocative of the power of her voice. They are, roughly, "loud and super-loud," from *gáirech*, "noisy, clamorous, loud, roaring."[280] Interestingly, that word shares the root *gair*, with verbs for calling, summoning, invoking, and proclaiming.[281] This seems to be a bit of *Dindshenchas* lore here, referencing not only the deadly power of Némain's voice, but perhaps also the hero's shout that seems to evoke her presence.

In discussing this epithet, a veteran of both combat and anti-police action shared these insights about the impact of sound on the body and spirit: "I think about being under bombardment and how beyond the kinetic effect there is the shock and heart crushing assault of sound in all frequencies. How fear starts down in your belly and rises up and takes hold of you and you sweat and your breathing becomes shallow and difficult and you can't order your thoughts."[282]

In a fascinating example of Classical entities being re-imagined as Irish war goddesses, this epithet comes from *Togail na Tebe* which is a medieval Irish version of the *Thebaid of Statius*. In this text the Classical deities Tisiphone, Bellona, and Enyo are all reframed through the Irish lens. Here, it is Enyo who is responding to the ferocity of the combatants in a battle: "Such was the strength and pressure that each of them exerted on the other at that time that between them arose the warlike disturbing wife of Néit, to wit, Enyo, sister of Mars, the god of war."[283]

The Irish text is what points toward Némain: *in bé néit badba buaidirthi*. *Bé Néit* is often translated as "wife of Néit," and seen as a title for one or more of the war goddesses; however, since *néit* means "battle," it can also be read as "woman of battle."[284] If it is read as a title, "the wife of Néit," it points toward Némain, since she most commonly appears as the wife of Néit, although Badb occasionally does also. If it is read as a description, it could be any of the war goddesses. Whoever she is, she is *badba*, "warlike, violent, pertaining to battle," and *buaidirthi*, "disturbing, troubling, harassing, stirring-up" (as in making water muddy or turbid).[285]

The violent, harassing woman of battle, the warlike, battle-inciting wife of Néit, who stirs up confusion and chaos.

She of the wounds of war

For this epithet, I turn to *The Metrical Dindshenchas*, where a series of poems about Ailech Néit describe how Némain lived there with Néit: "Neit, son of Indui, his mother's brother, possessed Ailech, with Nemain, his law-giver wife, of the wounds of war."[286]

It's interesting to contemplate whether she is a cause or giver of wounds, or whether she herself carries wounds, or in some way wounds earned in battle are sacred to her. The phrase is *na cned cathach*, "battle-wounds" or "warlike wounds." There is, however, a secondary meaning of *cathach* when used as a substantive, where it denotes a sacred object or relic carried into battle for protection.[287] One could contemplate the scars of battle as marks of survival, sacred to the war goddess and perhaps carrying something of her protection with them.

Also, while the language here is what you'd expect for speaking of physical wounds, Némain's connection with battlefield terror does make me think of the mental wounds of war too—the horror and post-traumatic distress that can stay with a person as an invisible wound. For me, the shrieking of her voice also evokes a cathartic wailing or keening that can sometimes be part of processing trauma. She is the agent of battlefield terror, but in that I think she also understands its deep impacts.

The poem may be pointing to another aspect of Némain's relationship to war. In community discussions on the Litany, Caróg Liath pointed out that the verse seems to juxtapose "law giver" and "of the wounds of war," as if a connection between the two might have been intended.[288] This might point toward early Irish social customs about the honor price, the compensation owed for injuring or killing a person. Wounds of war incurred in battle could sometimes be considered legal injury and not subject to honor price in the way that acts of interpersonal violence would be. The legal status of war injuries might depend on the status of treaties between tribes or kingdoms.[289] Thus, the poem might allude to Némain being framed as a law-speaker on these issues of war-wounds and inter-tribal diplomacy.

Also from the series of *Dindshenchas* poems about Ailech Néit comes this epithet: "Neit son of Indui, the stranger, he of the long weapon, came and brought with him the winsome woman who dwelt in Brega: one like Nemain was never brought to the house of Ailech."[290] If you're like me, this word "winsome" might seem surprising to describe Némain. It conjures up the prim women in Edwardian dress catalogs—it has a connotation of someone who is pleasant, attractive, agreeable, and even sweet.

The Irish word is *builid*, which is a flexible word connoting beautiful, graceful, and praiseworthy.[291] One of its main use senses is applied to poetry, where it means "laudatory," that is, praise-poetry. This is interesting in that another of the *Dindshenchas* verses associates her with poetry. I see this epithet as highlighting her nobility, grace, and perhaps also her eloquence. One like her was never seen at that place before: she is unique and worthy of praise.

Wild and grim

This phrase appears in a *Metrical Dindshenchas* poem describing the fortress of Ailech where Némain lived: "Ailech Imchell was above every place a right sharp-crested stronghold, all-envied, among the Folk of Danu wild and grim, the precinct where dwelt Nemain and Neit."[292] This description, "wild and grim," seems to be speaking of the Túatha Dé Danann as a group, including Némain and Néit, as well as the "sharp-crested stronghold" that was their home. I've used it as an epithet in the litany as I feel it's in character with "warlike, disturbing" Némain.

The descriptive phrase "wild and grim" comes from *dremuin duairc*. *Dremun* is "furious, frantic, vigorous," a word that conjures wild, frenetic activity.[293] It's the same word which has been used to describe the Morrígan furiously washing the entrails of the dead. It suggests fierce, kinetic energy. *Dúairc* is "grim, stern, dire, gloomy, threatening."[294] It's an evocative portrait of fierce Némain and her consort: dire and frightful, filled with a wild energy that unleashes itself on the battlefield.

This unique epithet appears in a poem in the *Lebor Gabála Érenn*, praising the powerful women of the Túatha Dé Danann. Macalister's translation reads:

> *Neman of ingenious versicles,*
> *Danann, mother of the gods.*
> *Badb and Macha, greatness of wealth,*
> *Morrigu—springs of craftiness…*[295]

The Irish description of Némain is *na forand fathach*. She is associated with *forand*, a verse or division of poetry such as a quatrain.[296] Macalister translates this word as "versicles," but in English this word has a connotation of church liturgy, so I chose "verses" as a more neutral term in the Litany. Némain is also described as *fáthach*, possessing wisdom, skill, or knowledge; with a connotation of mystical or prophetic knowledge.[297] This passage associates Némain with wise, mystical or prophetic poetry and seems to be in the role of poetess, a role that the tradition more usually ascribes to the Morrígan or Badb.

Another consideration is that Irish poetry is very alliterative, often intentionally choosing words whose sounds will conjure another word in the mind of the listener, so as to convey multiple layers of meaning. With that in mind, I wonder whether the author also intended to allude to *forrán*, "violent aggression, assault, outburst."[298] The phrase would be evoking something like "Némain of the mystical attacks," which reminds me of her terrifying attacks in which warriors fell dead from the sound of her voice. This reading could suggest her acting on two levels at once— through both poetry and through her impact in the battlefield.

As with much of the material about Némain, this comes from the *Metrical Dindshenchas* poems about Ailech: "Neit, son of Indui, his mother's brother, possessed Ailech, with Nemain, his law-giver wife, of the wounds of war."[299] This translation comes across fairly directly from the Irish phrase *Nemain a ben brethach*. The adjective *brethach* is "judicial, pertaining to judgement," so "law-giver" is just a slightly more poetic turn of phrase here.[300]

It's worth noting that women in a judicial role are not common in Irish literature, so this is distinctive. The role is connected with the poetic skill referenced in the previous epithet, since in early Ireland, verse was used by judicial poets to enable memorization of the necessary large volumes of knowledge pertaining to law and judgment. Contrast this with the Morrígan's role as a poet, as she is described as an illegal satirist—one who performs magically weaponized poetry outside the constraints of the legal system and therefore considered renegade and quite dangerous. In contrast, Némain seems to be set up as a law-speaker poet, one who speaks with the voice of the judicial system. Both types of poets were held in a degree of awe, being understood to carry the power of the Otherworld and the ability to raise up or destroy people with their verses.

Némain's last epithet comes from another *Metrical Dindshenchas* poem about a place called Fich Buana. It tells a story of the place taking its name from Buan, a woman who offers marriage to Cú Chulainn.[301] It's an intriguing story in its own right, placing Buan into a story of the heroes' competition for the champion's portion. This may be a folk variant of the woman known as Buan's daughter, a guise the Morrígan takes in the *Táin* in order to distract Cú Chulainn by offering marriage.[302] Setting that comparison aside, this *Dindshenchas* tale is set at a place named for Némain, which is called "Fich Nemain of the anguish-cry," until Buan meets her death there and gives a new name to the place.

The Irish phrase is *Fích Nemain in núall-gáid*. A *fích* is a rural district or area of land, a loanword from Latin *vicus*.[303] However, I can't help wondering if this is an example of poetic language use that's meant to evoke a similar sounding word, because there is a second meaning of *fích* as "wrath, enmity, anger," appearing in phrases such as *fíochnimh*, "venomous wrath."[304] So it's "Némain's district," but perhaps also "Némain's wrath."

The cry of anguish is connected to this place before Buan is killed, which suggests to me that it's connected with Némain. It's a rather obscure phrase, but seems to be constructed from *úall*, "wailing, lamentation," or the related term *núall*, "loud noise."[305] The descriptor is *gád*, "danger, stress, need," which takes on a sense of "dire, perilous" in adjectival forms.[306] All these variant forms seem redolent of Némain: a great wailing or terrible loud noise which is dire and dangerous.

While Némain herself doesn't appear in this story, this phrase used to describe a landscape in her name seems very evocative of her character. Alternate readings could be, "Nemain's district of the dire lamentation," or "Némain's wrath of destructive outcry."

Daughters
of Ernmas

Most texts that mention the goddesses in the Morrígna group present them as daughters of an ancestral goddess Ernmas. In this closing section of the Litany, I have included epithets that are attached to the daughters of Ernmas as a collective.

This first one comes from two verses of a poem in the *Lebor Gabála Érenn*. Macalister's translation is the one that many readers may have seen:

Eriu, though it should reach a road-end,
Banba, Fotla, and Fea,
Neman of ingenious versicles,
Danann, mother of the gods.
Badb and Macha, greatness of wealth,
Morrigu—springs of craftiness,
sources of bitter fighting
were the three daughters of Ernmas.[307]

Macalister's translation just gives "three daughters," but Hennessy opts for "noble daughters."[308] Looking at the Irish text, it has *ingena ana Ernmais*; the descriptive word is *án* which has a range of meanings: relating to light and brightness, "fiery, bright, glowing," more generally "splendid, glorious."[309] It is also used as a comparative or superlative in the sense of "best, finest, most noble." The daughters of Ernmas are just the utmost: brilliant, glorious, radiant, the best of the best.

This might also be the place to discuss just how many daughters of Ernmas there are. Questions often arise around this poem which appears to list nine women as the "three daughters of Ernmas." It turns out the poem doesn't actually say "three daughters" at all! Macalister added that in his translation. But he didn't pull it out of nowhere. "Three daughters of Ernmas" is a motif that occurs often in the *LGE* material. For example, Badb, Macha, and Morrigu are designated this way in another part of the text, as are Eriu, Fotla, and Banba.[310] The medieval authors weren't confused about whether nine is different from three. What's happening here is that of the many daughters of Ernmas, some of them exist in triads that share a collective function, like the three war goddesses and the three sovereignty goddesses. In some places, this triadic nature is being highlighted, and in others, such as the above poem, the whole group is the focus.

From the same poem in the previous epithet, this next one comes also. It is from this verse:

Badb and Macha, greatness of wealth,
Morrigu—springs of craftiness,
sources of bitter fighting
were the three daughters of Ernmas.[311]

It is a little ambiguous as to whether the phrase is intended to describe the Morrígan as an individual or whether it is about the daughters of Ernmas as a group. Since it can also be translated in a variety of ways, I have made use of different interpretations of it both here and in the Morrígan's section of the Litany.

To recap the translation, the phrase comes from the Irish phrase *fotha felbais*, or in another manuscript version it's spelled *fatha felbais*.[312] *Fotha* is "foundation, origin, source, or cause;" or with the *fatha* spelling it would be "sovereignty, realm, pre-eminence."[313] The second part, *felmas* is "enchantment, sorcery; a charm or spell."[314] Macalister has "springs of craftiness," attributing it to the daughters of Ernmas as a group rather than specifically the Morrígan.[315] The language is rich with many allusions and meanings. It speaks to the daughters of Ernmas as sorceress prophetesses, or in a more mystical sense as a great wellspring or source from which sorcery and enchantments flow.

For this epithet, its source is a gloss in *Cormac's Glossary*. It is just a few words which bring up some very intriguing questions. The entry is a gloss on the word *gúdemain*, which is composed of the prefix *gú*, "false, lying," and *demain* which is a loanword from church Latin *daemon*, "demon, evil spirit."[316] In turn, *daemon* itself was originally a loan-word from Greek *daimon*, "deity, divine power, lesser god, or spirit."[317] Thus, *gúdemain* is a kind of window into the way in which older spirit beings were reclassified as demons in medieval Christian cosmology.

This word has been glossed in order to explain its meaning to a medieval audience. The gloss reads: *Gúdemain .i. úatha 7 morrígnae*. Borsje translates the gloss as "False demons, that is: terrors and Morrígnae."[318] John O'Donovan's older translation gives the descriptive phrase as "spectres and fairy queens."[319] The first part of the description, *úatha*, is one which has come up before; it is a "horror," a frightening phantom or spirit being, often associated with the Otherworld and the unquiet dead.[320] The second part is a generic or plural of Morrígan, "great queens" or perhaps "spectral queens." Similar entries appear in other glossaries, such as one that glosses *gúdemain* as "scald crows or women of the *síd.*"[321] These are part of a wider pattern framing the war goddesses as part of a collective of fearful spirit beings, perceived as "false demons" within a Christian cosmology.

What I take from this epithet is the sense of the daughters of Ernmas as part of a family of fearsome Otherworld spirits. The terror they seem to have represented for these authors speaks to the power these divinities were felt to have, a power which Christian cosmology eventually had no place for other than to classify it as demonic.

Compassers of death by the sword

This epithet returns to the praise poem from the *Lebor Gabála Érenn*. Speaking of Badb, Macha, and the Morrígan, it gives:

Indlema ind aga ernbais,
Ingena ana Ernmais.[322]

This is one of several manuscript versions with slight differences in the language, and Macalister doesn't translate this particular version. The translation I've used in the epithet comes from Hennessy, an antiquated work but one that I think is accurate here: "Compassers of death by the sword, Noble daughters of Ernmas."[323] Here the verb is *indlid*, "arrange, impose, prepare, especially in sense of preparing for battle," though it also has a use in speaking of composing poetry.[324] What they are bringing about is *aga ernbais*, a phrase composed of *ág*, "battle, strife, slaughter," and a compound word *ernbás*, made up of *íarn*, "iron, sword, weapon," and *bás*, "death."[325] That word *ernbás* is an idiom for "death by the sword," that is to say, violent death—but notice that it is also the root of Ernmas's name, the mother of these war goddesses, and it was clearly chosen both to rhyme with and to highlight Ernmas's name in the next line. This line reads as "they who bring about slaughter by the sword," but in a mythic sense it also says, "they who bring to fruition the power of Ernmas." It seems to suggest that Ernmas is violent death itself, and her daughters are the goddesses of battle who bring it about.

There is an alternate manuscript version of this poem which gives a different reading of the line, It appears a little later in this same section of the Litany, "Sources of bitter fighting."

There are quite a number of places where the Morrígna god-desses are described as crows of battle, which could be point-ed to as the source of this epithet. Many of these have already been presented in other epithets. One that I haven't yet discussed is in a glossary on a text called *Bretha Nemed Déidenach*.[326] In a gloss on *gúdemain*, "false demons," these are explained as "scald crows or women of the *síd*." This gloss is then further explained in a margin note as "the false demons, the Morrígna." The Mor-rígna as a collective are linked here to scald crows, demons, and fairy women or banshees.

The word used for "scald crows" is *fennóga*. This is a more specific term than *badb*, which can point to crows in general, or other supernatural beings. A *feannóg* specifies what is nowadays usually called a hooded crow (*Corvus cornix*), a species which is widespread in Ireland and would have often been seen about bat-tlefields.[327] Hooded crows are ashy gray on the body, with black on the head, wings, and tail, giving it a look as if wearing a black hood—perhaps contributing to its association with beings of war and deathly omen like the Morrígna.

By whose shrieks
a hundred warriors die of terror

This epithet returns to the theme of the destructive, terrifying power of the voices of the war goddesses. It originates from a passage in the *Táin Bó Cúailnge* which has already shown up in the Litany section for Némain. O'Rahilly's translation from the First Recension version reads, "But as for the men of Ireland, Badb and Bé Néit and Némain shrieked above them that night in Gáirech and Irgáirech so that a hundred of their warriors died of terror. That was not the most peaceful night for them."[328]

What happens to these warriors is a phenomenon called *úathbás*—literally, "horror-death."[329] It's a word that is occasionally used to describe an extreme state of shock, horror, or amazement, or just a severely heightened state of fear. In this story, it's presented as occurring literally—the warriors falling dead from their terror. Recalling also that *úath* is both the emotion of horror, and the spirit beings, "horrors," that cause it, this language conjures an incredibly visceral image of otherwise sturdy warriors shattered by abject terror of the spectral host raised by the shrieks of the war goddesses, a horror that grips them physically and stops their hearts.

The phrase "daughters of Ernmas" doesn't appear here, but since it is a group of three war goddesses who are usually presented as her daughters, it seems appropriate in their Litany. This behavior of shrieking over an army to terrify and kill is more usually associated with Némain in particular, but here they engage in it collectively. It's perhaps another example of the fluidity that these goddesses often demonstrate between their different identities, powers, and specializations.

Sources of bitter fighting

This epithet returns to the praise poem for the daughters of Ernmas in the *Lebor Gabála Érenn*. One version of this line appeared in the epithet, "Compassers of death by the sword." This present epithet takes its source from another manuscript variant of the same poem, where the line has different language. The Irish reads: *tindrema aga amnuis*.[330] Macalister's translation gives "sources of bitter fighting," which I've used in this epithet. Koch and Carey give "the guides of savage battle."[331]

It is a subtle difference of emphasis. Where the earlier rendition focuses intensely on the image of iron-death, echoed in Ernmas's name, this version conjures the roughness and cruelty of battlefield violence. The descriptor is *amnas*, "hard, rough, cruel," with a secondary sense of "keen, clever, cunning."[332] It carries the sense of a bitter, hard-fought conflict, perhaps one that requires great endurance and cunning to prevail. There is perhaps a sense of testing or harsh ordeal brought about by the daughters of Ernmas.

The daughters of Ernmas are mentioned in the role of sorceresses for the Túatha Dé Danann in a couple of places. The primary source for this epithet is a passage in the *Banshenchus*, a medieval text about important women in Irish myth and history. Maighréad Dobbs' translation gives: "Nemain, Danand, Bodb and Macha, Morrigu who brings victory, impetuous and swift Etain, Be Chuilli of the north country, were the sorceresses of the Tuatha De."[333] Elsewhere, the sorceresses Badb, Macha, and the Morrígan are described mustering in the vanguard of the Túatha Dé Danann to the first Battle of Mag Tuired.[334]

The word describing their role, translated as "sorceress" is *ban-túathech*. Its root is *túath*, a word which represents a complex of ideas like witchcraft, sorcery, danger, left-handedness, the northerly direction, and the evil eye—all things associated with the Otherworld.[335] *Túathech* is someone who wields these powers, i.e. a sorcerer, and the prefix *ban* indicates a woman practitioner.

There also seems to be a play on words happening in the *Banshenchus* text, because the word *túath* has two meanings. Apart from all of the above, it also means "a people or nation," as well as the country or kingdom they occupy, and was the basic territorial unit in the medieval period.[336] This phrase *ban-túathecha Túathe De Danand*, brings both these sets of meanings together. For a native speaker, this play on words would be obvious. It may be meant to highlight the idea of the Túatha Dé Danann as spooky and powerful, and these goddesses the spookiest of them all. This plays into a recurring motif about the Túatha Dé as being witchy and associated with magic and mystery, which appears throughout the Mythological Cycle texts. Scholar Mark Williams has pointed out that in part, this is a reframing performed by the medieval authors who set these stories into manuscript form. To justify preserving their lore in a time when pagan gods were seen as antithetical to the faith, medieval Christian scholars needed to reframe the Túatha Dé Danann as not being gods at all, but simply ancient people with occult powers.[337] Whereas in their pre-Christian cultural context, these powers would have been understood in a more religious, and less "spooky" sense as simply the holy powers of the gods.

It's interesting to reflect on how it might have come to be that the daughters of Ernmas, war goddesses, would especially carry this spooky, sorcerous image. In part, of course, it pertains to the actual powers that they wield, and their association with specters and Otherworld powers. I suspect it also reflects the difficulty that Christian theologians had in finding a place to safely incorporate these intimidating goddesses. Where some pagan gods could easily be folded into the lore of saints and holy prophets, the daughters of Ernmas stand apart, uncompromisingly fierce and wild, inseparable from the animistic, enspirited pagan world that birthed them.

Endnotes

1. Leahy, A H. Heroic Romances of Ireland, Vol II. Edinburgh & London: Ballantyne, Hanson & Co., 1906, 136.
2. eDIL 2019: An Electronic Dictionary of the Irish Language. Dublin: Royal Irish Academy, 2019, s.v. 1 síd, síth, http://www.dil.ie/37441.
3. See Kane for a detailed exploration of all these creatures. Kane, Catherine Helen. Emerging from the Cave: A Study of the Cave or Síd of Crúachan in Early Irish Literature. National University of Ireland, Cork, 2016.
4. Meyer, Kuno. The Triads of Ireland. Dublin: Hodges, Figgis, & Co., Ltd., 1906, 4.
5. Gwynn, Edward. "The Metrical Dindshenchas Volume 4." CELT: Corpus of Electronic Texts, 2008, 196. https://celt.ucc.ie/published/T106500D/index.html.
6. eDIL s.v. 1 samla, dil.ie/36146.
7. eDIL s.v. soïd, dil.ie/38322.
8. My adaptation based on Carmody, Isolde. "Rosc from Táin Bó Regamna." Unpublished translation, 2014.
9. Meyer, Kuno. Fianaigecht. Dublin: Hodges, Figgis & Co. Ltd., 1910, 74.
10. For a thorough look at these creatures, see Borsje, Jacqueline. "Omens, Ordeals and Oracles: On Demons and Weapons in Early Irish Texts." Peritia: Journal of the Medieval Academy of Ireland 13 (1999): 224–48.
11. eDIL s.v. mór, már, dil.ie/32548; eDIL s.v. rígain, rígan, dil.ie/35271.
12. Beck, Noémie. Goddesses in Celtic Religion—Cult and Mythology: A Comparative Study of Ancient Ireland, Britain and Gaul. Université Lumière Lyon, 2009, 262.
13. Gwynn, Metrical Dindshenchas Volume 4, 199.
14. eDIL s.v. mórda, dil.ie/32565.
15. Gray, Elizabeth A. "Cath Maige Tuired: The Second Battle of Mag Tuired." CELT: Corpus of Electronic Texts, 2003, 53. http://www.ucc.ie/celt/published/T300010.html.
16. Daimler, Morgan. "A Bit More Translation." Living Liminally, 2015. https://lairbhan.blogspot.com/2015/03/a-bit-more-translation.html.
17. eDIL s.v. 2 díbaid, dil.ie/15992; eDIL s.v. srían, dil.ie/38811.
18. Leahy, Heroic Romances, Vol II, 132.
19. Kelly, Fergus. A Guide to Early Irish Law. Dublin: Dublin Institute for Advanced Studies, 2003, 49-50.
20. Leahy, Heroic Romances, Vol II, 132.
21. eDIL s.v. rúad, dil.ie/35614.
22. eDIL s.v. derg, dil.ie/15626.
23. Gwynn, Metrical Dindshenchas Volume 4, 201.
24. eDIL s.v. ag, dil.ie/671.
25. eDIL s.v. ágdae, dil.ie/696.
26. Stokes, Whitley. "The Bodleian Dinnshenchas." Folklore 3 (1892): 471.
27. Meyer, Kuno. "The Adventures of Nera." Revue Celtique 10 (1889): 212–28.
28. O'Rahilly, Cecile. "Táin Bó Cúalnge Recension 1." CELT: Corpus of Electronic Texts, 2011, 176. http://www.ucc.ie/celt/published/T301012/index.html.
29. eDIL s.v. 1 derscaigthe, dil.ie/15718.
30. O'Rahilly, Cecile. "Táin Bó Cúalnge from the Book of Leinster." CELT: Corpus

of Electronic Texts, 2010, 194. https://celt.ucc.ie/published/T301035/.

31 O'Rahilly, Táin Bó Cúalnge Recension 1, 177.
32 Irish Moiled Cattle Society. "Breed History." The Irish Moiled Cattle Society, 2020. http://www.irishmoiledcattlesociety.com/breed-history/.
33 Ó Duinn, Sean. "The Siege of Knocklong." CELT: Corpus of Electronic Texts, 2014, 47. http://www.ucc.ie/celt/published/T301044/.
34 Gray, Cath Maige Tuired, 53.
35 Caróg Liath, Discord post, 5/11/2020. eDIL s.v. ar-sissedar, dil.ie/4312.
36 eDIL s.v. do-seinn, dil.ie/18453.
37 Gray, Cath Maige Tuired, 65.
38 Meyer, Fianaigecht, 17.
39 Fraser, J. "The First Battle of Moytura." Ériu 8 (1916): 43; O'Rahilly, Táin Bó Cúalnge Leinster, 150.
40 O'Rahilly, Táin Bó Cúalnge Recension 1, 152.
41 eDIL s.v. 2 áige, dil.ie/917.
42 eDIL s.v. óice, dil.ie/33614.
43 eDIL s.v. 1 bil, dil.ie/5877.
44 Gray, Cath Maige Tuired, 45.
45 eDIL s.v. trilis, dil.ie/41933.
46 eDIL s.v. do-aithbig, dil.ie/17164.
47 Meyer, Fianaigecht, xii.
48 Leahy, Heroic Romances, Vol II, 136.
49 eDIL s.v. dolud, dolaid, dil.ie/18049.
50 For more on this, see earlier section "Woman poet".
51 eDIL s.v. 1 grellach, dil.ie/26586.
52 eDIL s.v. slóg, slúag, dil.ie/37981.
53 eDIL s.v. dírmach, dil.ie/16746.
54 eDIL s.v. sámda, dil.ie/36139.
55 Rob Preece, Discord post, 05/15/2020.
56 O'Rahilly, Táin Bó Cúalnge Recension 1, 181.
57 eDIL s.v. sentonn, dil.ie/37180; eDIL s.v. caillech, dil.ie/7751.
58 eDIL s.v. cáech, dil.ie/7571.
59 eDIL s.v. losc, dil.ie/30704.
60 Gwynn, Metrical Dindshenchas Volume 4, 199.
61 eDIL s.v. fiach, dil.ie/21873.
62 eDIL s.v. 3 aire, dil.ie/1885.
63 eDIL s.v. fíachaire, dil.ie/21879.
64 eDIL s.v. fíachairecht, dil.ie/21880.
65 eDIL s.v. fáthach, dil.ie/21360.
66 Foras na Gaeilge. "Teanglann.Ie," 2022, https://www.teanglann.ie/en/fgb/fia-chaire.
67 Macalister, R. A. S. Lebor Gabála Érenn: The Book of the Taking of Ireland, Part IV. Dublin: Irish Texts Society, 1941, 189.
68 Fraser, First Battle of Moytura, 45.
69 eDIL s.v. 1 delb, dil.ie/15324.
70 Williams, Mark. Ireland's Immortals: A History of the Gods of Irish Myth. Princeton, New Jersey: Princeton University Press, 2016, 161.

71 See epithet "Compassers of death by the sword," in the last section of the Litany, for more about Ernmas.

72 Leahy, Heroic Romances, Vol II, 136.

73 eDIL s.v. 1 én, dil.ie/20038.

74 eDIL s.v. dub, dil.ie/18985.

75 O'Donovan, John. "The Banquet of Dun Na N-Gedh and the Battle of Magh Rath." Irish Archaeological Society 6 (1842), 199.

76 eDIL s.v. caillech, dil.ie/7751.

77 eDIL s.v. lomm, dil.ie/30602.

78 eDIL s.v. 1 lúath, dil.ie/30854; eDIL s.v. 2 léimnech, dil.ie/29800.

79 eDIL s.v. mong, dil.ie/32532.

80 Stokes, Whitley. "The Destruction of Da Derga's Hostel." CELT: Corpus of Electronic Texts, 2009, http://www.ucc.ie/celt/published/T301017A/index.html; Stokes, Whitley. "Da Choca's Hostel." Revue Celtique 21 (1900): 149–75, 312–28, 388–404.

81 Shannon Thompson, Discord post, 5/22/2020.

82 Koch, John T., and John Carey. The Celtic Heroic Age: Literary Sources for Ancient Celtic Europe and Early Ireland & Wales. Aberystwyth: Celtic Studies Publications, 2003, 255.

83 eDIL s.v. 1 fotha, dil.ie/24155.

84 Macalister, Lebor Gabála Érenn, Part IV, 216-217.

85 eDIL s.v. 1 flaith, dil.ie/22281.

86 eDIL s.v. felmas, dil.ie/21572.

87 Macalister, Lebor Gabála Érenn, Part IV, 217.

88 Hennessy, William M. "The Ancient Irish Goddess of War." Revue Celtique I (1872): 37.

89 Gwynn, Metrical Dindshenchas Volume 4, 201.

90 eDIL s.v. úathmar, dil.ie/42831.

91 eDIL s.v. 1 úath, dil.ie/42805.

92 eDIL s.v. cubaid, dil.ie/13383.

93 For an overview of the cave's creatures, see Waddell, John. "Rathcroghan—A Royal Site in Connacht." Journal of Irish Archaeology 1 (1983): 21–46.

94 Meyer, Fianaigecht, 16-17.

95 eDIL s.v. dremun, dil.ie/18637.

96 eDIL s.v. 1 cais, dil.ie/7955.

97 eDIL s.v. 1 gen, dil.ie/25635.

98 Borsje, Jacqueline. "The 'Terror of the Night' and the Morrígain: Shifting Faces of the Supernatural." In Proceedings of the Seventh Symposium of Societas Celtologica Nordica, edited by Mícheál Ó Flaithearta, 71–98. Uppsala: Acta Universitatis Upsaliensis, 2007, 83. Greene and O'Connor quoted in Borsje, 83, footnote 37.

99 Stokes, Whitley. "Cóir Anmann (Fitness of Names)." In Irische Text Mit Wörterbuch, 288–411. Leipzig: Verlag Von S. Hirzel, 1897, 149.

100 eDIL s.v. richt, dil.ie/35260.

101 Stokes, Whitley. "The Prose Tales in the Rennes Dindshenchas." Thesaurus Linguae Hibernicae, 2008. https://www.ucd.ie/tlh/trans/ws.rc.16.001.t.text.html.

102 eDIL s.v. 1 ben, dil.ie/5644.

103 Gwynn, Edward. "The Metrical Dindshenchas Volume 2." CELT: Corpus of Electronic Texts. CELT: Corpus of Electronic Texts: a project of University College, Cork, 2008, 11. http://www.ucc.ie/celt/published/T106500B/index.html.
104 eDIL s.v. lánamain, dil.ie/29545.
105 Gwynn, Metrical Dindshenchas Volume 2, 19.
106 eDIL s.v. rígain, rígan, dil.ie/35271.
107 O'Rahilly, Táin Bó Cúalnge Leinster, 194.
108 See for example Dúchas folklore site, keyword "eel": National Folklore Collection UCD. "The Schools' Collection." Dúchas, 2021. https://www.duchas.ie/en/src?q=eel&t=CbesStory.
109 Ó Duinn, Siege of Knocklong, 87.
110 Leahy, Heroic Romances, Vol II, 136.
111 Flynn, Peter. "Táin Bó Regamna." CELT: Corpus of Electronic Texts, 2010, 32. http://www.ucc.ie/celt/online/G301005/.
112 Epstein, Angelique Gulermovich. War Goddess: The Morrígan and Her Germano-Celtic Counterparts. Los Angeles: University of California, 1998, 129-130.
113 eDIL s.v. 3 díden, dil.ie/16217; eDIL s.v. dítiu, dil.ie/16919.
114 See previous discussions on the heifer and eel shapes.
115 O'Rahilly, Táin Bó Cúalnge Leinster, 194.
116 eDIL s.v. sod, sad, dil.ie/38276.
117 O'Rahilly, Táin Bó Cúalnge Recension 1, 61.
118 eDIL s.v. 1 garb, dil.ie/25380/.
119 Stokes, Whitley. Acallamh Na Senórach. Edited by W.H. Stokes and E. Windisch. Leipzig: Verlag Von S. Hirzel, 1900, 264-266.
120 O'Rahilly, Táin Bó Cúalnge Leinster, 263.
121 eDIL s.v. indlach, dil.ie/28454; eDIL s.v. etarchossaít, dil.ie/20678.
122 O'Rahilly, Táin Bó Cúalnge Recension 1, 229.
123 O'Donovan, Battle of Magh Rath, 199.
124 eDIL s.v. 2 léimnech, dil.ie/29800.
125 For more on this, see Borsje, Omens, Ordeals and Oracles.
126 Meyer, Fianaigecht, 16-17.
127 eDIL s.v. 1 fodb, fadb, dil.ie/22569.
128 eDIL s.v. inathar, dil.ie/28229.
129 eDIL s.v. dímór, dil.ie/16559.
130 eDIL s.v. dremun, dil.ie/18637.
131 Gwynn, Metrical Dindshenchas Volume 4, 196-201.
132 eDIL s.v. tnúthach, dil.ie/41029.
133 eDIL s.v. 1 garb, dil.ie/25380; eDIL s.v. gnáthach, dil.ie/26194.
134 Dobbs, Maighréad ni C. "The Ban-Shenchus." Revue Celtique 47 (1930), 292, 318.
135 eDIL s.v. beirid, dil.ie/5583.
136 eDIL s.v. 1 búaid, dil.ie/7221.
137 Mees, Bernard. Celtic Curses. Kindle. Woodbridge: The Boydell Press, 2009, 145-146.
138 eDIL s.v. mong, dil.ie/32532.
139 O'Donovan, John. "Annals of the Four Masters." Edited by Emma Ryan. CELT: Corpus of Electronic Texts, 2002, 73. http://www.ucc.ie/celt/published/

T100005A/index.html.

140 Gwynn, Metrical Dindshenchas Volume 4, 124.

141 eDIL s.v. 1 menn, mend, dil.ie/31959.

142 eDIL s.v. mer, dil.ie/31981.

143 Toner, Gregory. "Macha and the Invention of Myth." Ériu 60 (2010): 105.

144 eDIL s.v. glicc, dil.ie/26087.

145 eDIL s.v. gliccus, dil.ie/26089.

146 O'Curry, Eugene. Lectures on the Manuscript Materials of Ancient Irish History. Dublin: James Duffy, 1861, 527-528; O'Donovan, Annals of the Four Masters, 73.

147 O'Curry, Lectures on the Manuscript Materials, 528.

148 Gwynn, Metrical Dindshenchas Volume 4, 124-131.

149 eDIL s.v. 2 gairge, dil.ie/25233.

150 eDIL s.v. 1 glóir, dil.ie/26118.

151 eDIL s.v. 2 glór, dil.ie/26142.

152 Macalister, R. A. S. Lebor Gabála Érenn: The Book of the Taking of Ireland, Part V. Dublin: Irish Texts Society, 1956, 461.

153 eDIL s.v. 1 úall, úaill, dil.ie/42708.

154 eDIL s.v. méit, mét, dil.ie/31852.

155 eDIL s.v. 3 úall, dil.ie/42710.

156 Gwynn, Metrical Dindshenchas Volume 4, 124-131.

157 Stokes, Whitley. "The Edinburgh Dinnshenchas." Folklore 4 (1893): 473–97, 481.

158 eDIL s.v. grían, dil.ie/26628.

159 Gwynn, Metrical Dindshenchas Volume 4, 308.

160 Gwynn, Metrical Dindshenchas Volume 4, 124; Stokes, Edinburgh Dinnshenchas, 481; Macalister, Lebor Gabála Érenn, Part III, 131; Dobbs, Ban-Shenchus, 317.

161 Macalister, Lebor Gabála Érenn, Part V, 57.

162 Macalister, Lebor Gabála Érenn, Part IV, 217

163 eDIL s.v. indmas, indbas, dil.ie/28489; eDIL s.v. méit, mét, dil.ie/31852.

164 eDIL s.v. 1 macha, machad, dil.ie/31192.

165 Gwynn, Metrical Dindshenchas Volume 4, 124.

166 eDIL s.v. bán, dil.ie/5318.

167 eDIL s.v. balar, dil.ie/5286.

168 Gwynn, Metrical Dindshenchas Volume 4, 124.

169 eDIL s.v. 1 ard, dil.ie/4041.

170 Gwynn, Metrical Dindshenchas Volume 4, 113.

171 Stokes, Cóir Anmann, 357.

172 Gwynn, Metrical Dindshenchas Volume 4, 124.

173 eDIL s.v. torrach, dil.ie/41487; eDIL s.v. balc, dil.ie/5293.

174 Gwynn, Metrical Dindshenchas Volume 4, 124.

175 eDIL s.v. berg, dil.ie/5705.

176 eDIL s.v. díberg, dil.ie/16020.

177 Stokes, Whitley. "O'Mulconry's Glossary." Archiv Fur Celtische Lexikographie 1 (1900): 232–324, 271.

178 eDIL s.v. mesrad, dil.ie/32072.

179 Meyer, Kuno. "The Wooing of Emer." Archaeological Review 1 (1888): 151.
180 Dobbs, Ban-Shenchus, 317.
181 eDIL s.v. mín, dil.ie/32283.
182 Gwynn, Metrical Dindshenchas Volume 4, 124.
183 eDIL s.v. 1 bráen, dil.ie/6469.
184 eDIL s.v. 1 búaid, dil.ie/7221.
185 eDIL s.v. badb, dil.ie/5114.
186 Fraser, First Battle of Moytura, 33.
187 O'Rahilly, Táin Bó Cúalnge Leinster, 248.
188 eDIL s.v. 1 úathach, dil.ie/42813; eDIL s.v. badb, dil.ie/5114.
189 Hennessy, Ancient Irish Goddess of War, 53.
190 O'Curry, Eugene. Cath Mhuighe Leana, or The Battle of Magh Leana; Together with Tocmarc Momera, or The Courtship of Momera. Dublin: Goodwin, Son, and Nethercott, 1855, 131.
191 eDIL s.v. gorm, dil.ie/26408.
192 Shercliff, Rebecca Mary. A Critical Edition of Tochmarc Ferbe with Translation, Textual Notes and Literary Commentary. University of Cambridge, 2018, 39.
193 Hennessy, Ancient Irish Goddess of War, 38.
194 eDIL s.v. ár, dil.ie/3912; eDIL s.v. slóg, slúag, dil.ie/37981.
195 O'Rahilly, Cecile. Tóruigheacht Gruaidhe Griansholus: The Pursuit of Gruaidh Ghriansholus. London: Irish Texts Society, 1924, 93.
196 Meyer, Fianaigecht, 94.
197 Leahy, A H. The Irish Saga Library, Vol. 1: The Courtship of Ferb. London: David Nutt, 1902, 41.
198 eDIL s.v. bán, dil.ie/5318.
199 Shercliff, Tochmarc Ferbe, 75.
200 eDIL s.v. bánad, dil.ie/5320.
201 O'Connor, Ralph. The Destruction of Da Derga's Hostel: Kingship and Narrative Artistry in a Mediaeval Irish Saga. Oxford: Oxford University Press, 2013,138.
202 eDIL s.v. feochair, dil.ie/21623.
203 Tymoczko, Maria. Two Death Tales from the Ulster Cycle: The Death of Cu Roi & The Death of Cu Chulainn. Dublin: The Dolmen Press, 1981, 49-50.
204 eDIL s.v. ammait, dil.ie/3165.
205 eDIL s.v. 2 túath-, dil.ie/42242; eDIL s.v. cáech, dil.ie/7571.
206 Van Hamel, A.G. Compert Con Culainn and Other Stories. Mediaeval. Dublin: The Stationery Office, 1933, 82.
207 Calder, George. Togail Na Tebe: The Thebaid of Statius. Cambridge: The University Press, 1922, 12-13.
208 eDIL s.v. bruthmar, dil.ie/7174.
209 eDIL s.v. bél, dil.ie/5607.
210 O'Rahilly, Táin Bó Cúalnge Recension 1, 187.
211 eDIL s.v. ríastrad, dil.ie/35242.
212 eDIL s.v. caindel, dil.ie/7800.
213 O'Rahilly, Táin Bó Cúalnge Leinster, 228.
214 For translation and analysis, see Borsje, Omens, Ordeals and Oracles.
215 eDIL s.v. demon, dil.ie/15433.

216 Harper, Douglas. "Online Etymology Dictionary," 2022. https://www.etymon-line.com/word/daemon.

217 Stokes, Whitley. "In Cath Catharda: The Civil War of the Romans." CELT: Corpus of Electronic Texts, 2010, 435. http://www.ucc.ie/celt/published/T305001/index.html.

218 eDIL s.v. aslach, dil.ie/4447; eDIL s.v. immairecc, immairg, dil.ie/27679.

219 Borsje, Terror of the Night, 85-86.

220 eDIL s.v. 1 tethra, dil.ie/40645.

221 Borsje, Terror of the Night, 86.

222 eDIL s.v. 1 teine, dil.ie/40385.

223 Macalister, Lebor Gabála Érenn, Part V, 538-539.

224 eDIL s.v. berach, dil.ie/5693.

225 Kelly, Early Irish Law, 50.

226 O'Connor, Destruction of Da Derga's Hostel, 136-137.

227 eDIL s.v. méide, dil.ie/31755.

228 O'Connor, Destruction of Da Derga's Hostel, 217.

229 O'Rahilly, Táin Bó Cúalnge Recension 1, 138.

230 eDIL s.v. cúlad, dil.ie/13752.

231 Stokes, Da Derga's Hostel, 70.

232 eDIL s.v. aidmilled, dil.ie/895.

233 O'Connor, Destruction of Da Derga's Hostel, 135-137.

234 eDIL s.v. sod, sad, dil.ie/38276.

235 Koch and Carey, The Celtic Heroic Age, 88.

236 eDIL s.v. badbda, dil.ie/5118.

237 eDIL s.v. 1 bárc, dil.ie/5400.

238 eDIL s.v. 1 bruth, dil.ie/7164; eDIL s.v. bráth, dil.ie/6579.

239 Stokes, Da Choca's Hostel, 157.

240 eDIL s.v. derg, dil.ie/15626.

241 eDIL s.v. 1 fonnad, dil.ie/23255; eDIL s.v. 1 fortche, dil.ie/23972; eDIL s.v. 1 fodb, fadb, dil.ie/22569.

242 O'Connor, Destruction of Da Derga's Hostel, 217.

243 eDIL s.v. ernbas, dil.ie/20311.

244 O'Connor, Destruction of Da Derga's Hostel, 218.

245 van der Sanden, Wijnand A. B. "Bog Bodies: Underwater Burials, Sacrifices, and Executions." In The Oxford Handbook of Wetland Archaeology, edited by Francesco Menotti and Aidan O'Sullivan, 401–16. Oxford: Oxford University Press, 2013, 407.

246 Heijda, Kim. War-Goddesses, Furies and Scald Crows: The Use of the Word Badb in Early Irish Literature. University of Utrecht, 2007, 46.

247 eDIL s.v. ár, dil.ie/3912.

248 eDIL s.v. slicht, dil.ie/37930.

249 O'Rahilly, Pursuit of Gruaidh Ghriansholus, 125.

250 eDIL s.v. cíccarach, dil.ie/9033.

251 eDIL s.v. crob, dil.ie/13030; eDIL s.v. derg, dil.ie/15626.

252 For more on this, see Armao, Frédéric. "Cathair Crobh Dearg: From Ancient Beliefs to the Rounds 2017." Estudios Irlandeses 12, no. 2 Special Issue (2017): 8–31; Coyne, Frank. Islands in the Clouds: An Upland Archaeological Study on

Mount Brandon and the Paps, County Kerry. Kerry County Council, 2006, 47.
253 Gray, Cath Maige Tuired, 71.
254 O'Rahilly, Táin Bó Cúalnge Recension 1, 202.
255 eDIL s.v. scaraid, dil.ie/36327.
256 O'Rahilly, Táin Bó Cúalnge Leinster, 77; eDIL s.v. 3 gairid, dil.ie/25237.
257 Kinsella, Thomas. The Táin: Translated from the Irish Epic Táin Bó Cúailnge. Oxford: Oxford University Press, 1969, 176; Carson, Ciaran. The Táin: A New Translation of the Táin Bó Cúailnge. London: Penguin Classics, 2007, 132.
258 O'Rahilly, Táin Bó Cúalnge Recension 1, 231.
259 O'Rahilly, Pursuit of Gruaidh Ghriansholus, 27.
260 Stokes, Whitley. "The Battle of Allen." Revue Celtique 24 (1903): 54.
261 eDIL s.v. berach, dil.ie/5693.
262 Shercliff, Tochmarc Ferbe, 39.
263 Shercliff, Tochmarc Ferbe, 54-55.
264 eDIL s.v. bán, dil.ie/5318.
265 eDIL s.v. builid, dil.ie/7387.
266 eDIL s.v. 1 lí, dil.ie/30091.
267 Shercliff, Tochmarc Ferbe, 55.
268 Shercliff, Tochmarc Ferbe, 75.
269 Shercliff, Tochmarc Ferbe, 39.
270 eDIL s.v. bris(s)id, dil.ie/6848.
271 eDIL s.v. nemain, dil.ie/33076.
272 eDIL s.v. neim, dil.ie/33028.
273 eDIL s.v. 1 nem, dil.ie/33070.
274 O'Donovan, John. Sanas Chormaic: Cormac's Glossary. Edited by John O'Donovan. Calcutta: O. T. Cutter, 1868, 26.
275 eDIL s.v. 1 neimnech, dil.ie/33041.
276 O'Rahilly, Táin Bó Cúalnge Recension 1, 231; Meyer, Wooing of Emer, 231; O'Donovan, Sanas Chormaic, 243.
277 eDIL s.v. 1 bé, dil.ie/5502.
278 O'Rahilly, Táin Bó Cúalnge Leinster, 197.
279 O'Rahilly, Táin Bó Cúalnge Recension 1, 231.
280 eDIL s.v. 1 gáirech, dil.ie/25221.
281 eDIL s.v. do-gair, dil.ie/17726.
282 Rob Preece, Discord post, 8/07/2020
283 Calder, Togail Na Tebe, 209.
284 eDIL s.v. néit, dil.ie/33059.
285 eDIL s.v. búaidrid, dil.ie/7230.
286 Gwynn, Metrical Dindshenchas Volume 4, 103.
287 eDIL s.v. 1 cathach, dil.ie/8347.
288 Caróg Liath, Discord post, 8/14/2020.
289 Kelly, Early Irish Law, 129.
290 Gwynn, Metrical Dindshenchas Volume 4, 115.
291 eDIL s.v. builid, dil.ie/7387.
292 Gwynn, Metrical Dindshenchas Volume 4, 96.
293 eDIL s.v. dremun, dil.ie/18637.
294 eDIL s.v. dúairc, dil.ie/18943.

295 Macalister, Lebor Gabála Érenn, Part IV, 217.
296 eDIL s.v. 2 rann, rand, dil.ie/34805.
297 eDIL s.v. fáthach, dil.ie/21360.
298 eDIL s.v. forrán, dil.ie/23857.
299 Gwynn, Metrical Dindshenchas Volume 4, 103.
300 eDIL s.v. brethach, dil.ie/6759.
301 Gwynn, Metrical Dindshenchas Volume 4, 181.
302 O'Rahilly, Táin Bó Cúalnge Recension 1, 176.
303 eDIL s.v. 1 fích, dil.ie/21974.
304 eDIL s.v. 2 fích, dil.ie/21975.
305 eDIL s.v. 3 úall, dil.ie/42710; eDIL s.v. 1 núall, dil.ie/33338.
306 eDIL s.v. gád, dil.ie/25071.
307 Macalister, Lebor Gabála Érenn, Part IV, 217.
308 Hennessy, Ancient Irish Goddess of War, 37.
309 eDIL s.v. 2 án, dil.ie/3242.
310 Macalister, Lebor Gabála Érenn, Part IV, 131.
311 Macalister, Lebor Gabála Érenn, Part IV, 217.
312 Macalister, Lebor Gabála Érenn, Part IV, 216-217.
313 eDIL s.v. 1 fotha, dil.ie/24155; eDIL s.v. 1 flaith, dil.ie/22281.
314 eDIL s.v. felmas, dil.ie/21572.
315 Macalister, Lebor Gabála Érenn, Part IV, 217.
316 eDIL s.v. gú-, dil.ie/26738; eDIL s.v. demon, dil.ie/15433.
317 Harper, Online Etymology Dictionary. https://www.etymonline.com/word/dae-mon.
318 Borsje, Terror of the Night, 82.
319 O'Donovan, Sanas Chormaic, 87.
320 eDIL s.v. 1 úath, dil.ie/42805.
321 Bretha Nemed déidenach, translated in Borsje, Terror of the Night, 88.
322 Macalister, Lebor Gabála Érenn, Part IV, 216.
323 Hennessy, Ancient Irish Goddess of War, 37.
324 eDIL s.v. indlid, dil.ie/28474.
325 eDIL s.v. 2 ág, dil.ie/673; eDIL s.v. íarn, dil.ie/27041; eDIL s.v. 1 bás, dil.ie/5444.
326 Borsje, Terror of the Night, 88.
327 eDIL s.v. fennóc, dil.ie/21617.
328 O'Rahilly, Táin Bó Cúalnge Recension 1, 231.
329 eDIL s.v. úathbás, úathfás, dil.ie/42825.
330 Macalister, Lebor Gabála Érenn, Part IV, 217.
331 Koch and Carey, The Celtic Heroic Age, 255.
332 eDIL s.v. amnas, dil.ie/3185.
333 Dobbs, Ban-Shenchus, 318.
334 Fraser, First Battle of Moytura, 45.
335 eDIL s.v. 2 túath-, dil.ie/42242.
336 eDIL s.v. 1 túath, dil.ie/42241.
337 Williams, Ireland's Immortals, 149-150.

Bibliography

Armao, Frédéric. "Cathair Crobh Dearg: From Ancient Beliefs to the Rounds 2017." *Estudios Irlandeses* 12, no. 2 Special Issue (2017): 8–31. https://doi.org/10.24162/EI2017-7511.

Beck, Noémie. Goddesses in Celtic Religion—Cult and Mythology: A Comparative Study of Ancient Ireland, Britain and Gaul. Université Lumière Lyon, 2009.

Borsje, Jacqueline. "Omens, Ordeals and Oracles: On Demons and Weapons in Early Irish Texts." *Peritia: Journal of the Medieval Academy of Ireland* 13 (1999): 224–48.

— "The 'Terror of the Night' and the Morrígain: Shifting Faces of the Supernatural." In *Proceedings of the Seventh Symposium of Societas Celtologica Nordica*, edited by Mícheál Ó Flaithearta, 71–98. Uppsala: Acta Universitatis Upsaliensis, 2007.

Calder, George. *Togail Na Tebe: The Thebaid of Statius*. Cambridge: The University Press, 1922.

Carmody, Isolde. "Rosc from Táin Bó Regamna." Unpublished translation, 2014.

Carson, Ciaran. The Táin: A New Translation of the Táin Bó Cúailnge. London: Penguin Classics, 2007.

Coyne, Frank. Islands in the Clouds: An Upland Archaeological Study on Mount Brandon and the Paps, County Kerry. Kerry County Council, 2006.

Daimler, Morgan. "A Bit More Translation." *Living Liminally*, 2015. https://lairbhan.blogspot.com/2015/03/a-bit-more-translation.html.

Dobbs, Maighréad ni C. "The Ban-Shenchus." *Revue Celtique* 47 (1930).

eDIL 2019. An Electronic Dictionary of the Irish Language. Dublin: Royal Irish Academy, 2019.

Epstein, Angelique Gulermovich. *War Goddess: The Morrígan and Her Germano-Celtic Counterparts*. Los Angeles: University of California, 1998.

Flynn, Peter. "Táin Bó Regamna." *CELT: Corpus of Electronic Texts*, 2010. http://www.ucc.ie/celt/online/G301005/.

Foras na Gaeilge. *Teanglann.ie*, 2022. https://www.teanglann.ie/en/.

Fraser, J. "The First Battle of Moytura." Ériu 8 (1916): 1–63.

Gray, Elizabeth A. "Cath Maige Tuired: The Second Battle of Mag Tuired." *CELT: Corpus of Electronic Texts*, 2003. http://www.ucc.ie/celt/published/T300010.html.

Gwynn, Edward. "The Metrical Dindshenchas Volume 2." *CELT: Corpus of Electronic Texts*, 2008. http://www.ucc.ie/celt/published/T106500B/index.html.

— "The Metrical Dindshenchas Volume 4." *CELT: Corpus of Electronic Texts*, 2008. https://celt.ucc.ie/published/T106500D/index.html.

Harper, Douglas. *Online Etymology Dictionary*, 2022. https://www.etymonline.com/.

Heijda, Kim. War-Goddesses, Furies and Scald Crows: The Use of the Word Badb in Early Irish Literature. University of Utrecht, 2007.

Hennessy, William M. "The Ancient Irish Goddess of War." *Revue Celtique* I (1872): 32–55.

Irish Moiled Cattle Society. "Breed History." *The Irish Moiled Cattle Society*, 2020. http://www.irishmoiledcattlesociety.com/breed-history/.

Kane, Catherine Helen. Emerging from the Cave: A Study of the Cave or Síd of Crúachan in Early Irish Literature. National University of Ireland, Cork, 2016.

Kelly, Fergus. *A Guide to Early Irish Law*. Dublin: Dublin Institute for Advanced Studies, 2003.

Kinsella, Thomas. *The Táin: Translated from the Irish Epic Táin Bó Cúailnge*. Oxford: Oxford University Press, 1969

Koch, John T., and John Carey. The Celtic Heroic Age: Literary Sources for Ancient Celtic Europe and Early Ireland & Wales. Aberystwyth: Celtic Studies Publications, 2003.

Leahy, A H. *Heroic Romances of Ireland*, Vol II. Edinburgh & London: Ballantyne, Hanson & Co., 1906.

— The Irish Saga Library, Vol. 1: The Courtship of Ferb. London: David Nutt, 1902.

Macalister, R. A. S. *Lebor Gabála Érenn: The Book of the Taking of Ireland*, Part IV. Dublin: Irish Texts Society, 1941.

— Lebor Gabála Érenn: The Book of the Taking of Ireland, Part V. Dublin: Irish Texts Society, 1956.

Mees, Bernard. *Celtic Curses*. Kindle. Woodbridge: The Boydell Press, 2009.

Meyer, Kuno. "The Adventures of Nera." *Revue Celtique* 10 (1889): 212–28.

— *Fianaigecht*. Dublin: Hodges, Figgis & Co. Ltd., 1910.

— *The Triads of Ireland*. Dublin: Hodges, Figgis, & Co., Ltd., 1906.

— "The Wooing of Emer." *Archaeological Review* 1 (1888): 68–75; 150–155; 231–235; 298–307.

National Folklore Collection UCD. "The Schools' Collection." *Dúchas*, 2021. https://www.duchas.ie/en.

O'Connor, Ralph. The Destruction of Da Derga's Hostel: Kingship and Narrative Artistry in a Mediaeval Irish Saga. Oxford: Oxford University Press, 2013.

O'Curry, Eugene. Cath Mhuighe Leana, or The Battle of Magh Leana; Together with Tocmarc Momera, or The Courtship of Momera. Dublin: Goodwin, Son, and Nethercott, 1855.

— Lectures on the Manuscript Materials of Ancient Irish History. Dublin: James Duffy, 1861.

O'Donovan, John. "Annals of the Four Masters." Edited by Emma Ryan. *CELT: Corpus of Electronic Texts*, 2002. http://www.ucc.ie/celt/published/T100005A/index.html.

— "The Banquet of Dun Na N-Gedh and the Battle of Magh Rath." *Irish Archaeological Society* 6 (1842).

— *Sanas Chormaic: Cormac's Glossary*. Calcutta: O. T. Cutter, 1868.

Ó Duinn, Sean. "The Siege of Knocklong." *CELT: Corpus of Electronic Texts*, 2014. http://www.ucc.ie/celt/published/T301044/.

O'Rahilly, Cecile. "Táin Bó Cúalnge from the Book of Leinster." *CELT: Corpus of Electronic Texts*, 2010. https://celt.ucc.ie/published/T301035/.

— "Táin Bó Cúalnge Recension 1." *CELT: Corpus of Electronic Texts*, 2011. http://www.ucc.ie/celt/published/T301012/index.html.

— Tóruigheacht Gruaidhe Griansholus: The Pursuit of Gruaidh Ghriansholus. London: Irish Texts Society, 1924.

Shercliff, Rebecca Mary. A Critical Edition of Tochmarc Ferbe with Translation, Textual Notes and Literary Commentary. University of Cambridge, 2018.

Stokes, Whitley. *Acallamh Na Senórach*. Edited by W.H. Stokes and E. Windisch. Leipzig: Verlag Von S. Hirzel, 1900.

— "The Battle of Allen." *Revue Celtique* 24 (1903): 41–67.

— "The Bodleian Dinnshenchas." *Folklore* 3 (1892): 467–516.

— "Cóir Anmann (Fitness of Names)." In *Irische Text Mit Wörterbuch*, 288–411. Leipzig: Verlag Von S. Hirzel, 1897.

— "Da Choca's Hostel." *Revue Celtique* 21 (1900): 149–75, 312–28, 388–404.

— "The Destruction of Da Derga's Hostel." *CELT: Corpus of Electronic Texts*, 2009. http://www.ucc.ie/celt/published/T301017A/index.html.

— "The Edinburgh Dinnshenchas." *Thesaurus Linguae Hibernicae*, 2007. https://www.ucd.ie/tlh/trans/ws.fl.4.001.t.text.html.

— "In Cath Catharda: The Civil War of the Romans." *CELT: Corpus of Electronic Texts*, 2010. http://www.ucc.ie/celt/published/T305001/index.html.

— "O'Mulconry's Glossary." *Archiv Fur Celtische Lexikographie* 1 (1900): 232–324.

— "The Prose Tales in the Rennes Dindshenchas." *Thesaurus Linguae Hibernicae*, 2008. https://www.ucd.ie/tlh/trans/ws.rc.16.001.t.text.html.

Toner, Gregory. "Macha and the Invention of Myth." Ériu 60 (2010): 81–109.

Tymoczko, Maria. Two Death Tales from the Ulster Cycle: The Death of Cu Roi & The Death of Cu Chulainn. Dublin: The Dolmen Press, 1981.

van der Sanden, Wijnand A. B. "Bog Bodies: Underwater Burials, Sacrifices, and Executions." In *The Oxford Handbook of Wetland Archaeology*, edited by Francesco Menotti and Aidan O'Sullivan, 401–16. Oxford: Oxford University Press, 2013.

Van Hamel, A.G. *Compert Con Culainn and Other Stories*. Dublin: The Stationery Office, 1933.

Waddell, John. "Rathcroghan—A Royal Site in Connacht." *Journal of Irish Archaeology* 1 (1983): 21–46.

Williams, Mark. *Ireland's Immortals: A History of the Gods of Irish Myth*. Princeton, New Jersey: Princeton University Press, 2016.

About the Author

Morpheus Ravenna is a genderfluid sorcerer, artist, and writer, residing in the East Bay area of California. Sí is a dedicant of the Morrígan, with a practice rooted in animism, folk magic, and Celtic polytheism. An initiate of the Anderson Feri tradition of witchcraft, sí has practiced devotional polytheism and the magical arts for over twenty-five years. Sí is the author of *The Book of the Great Queen*, available from Concrescent Press, and a priest and co-founder of the *Coru Cathubodua Priesthood*.

Morpheus makes hir living as a tattoo artist, and sí creates devotional artworks and sorcerous crafts in a variety of media. Sí also practices medieval armored combat and is very fond of spears. Morpheus can be reached through hir website at bansheearts.com.

About Concrescent Press

Concrescent Press is dedicated to publishing advanced magickal practice and Pagan scholarship. We take advantage of the recent revolution in publishing technology and economics to bring forth works that, previously, might only have been circulated privately. We are especially interested in publishing works like this one, focusing on the way and practice of invoking a Deity or set thereof. It is time to rebuild the temples, altars, and rites of the Gods, to bring back our communion with Them and Their many benefits into our world and lives.

Now, we are growing the future together.

Colophon

This book is made of Adobe Garamond Pro, Dumbledor, and Uncial Antiqua, using Adobe InDesign. Typography and book design by Sam Webster. All line art by Morpheus Ravenna,

Visit our website at
Concrescent.net